GRIEF
LIGHT

Other Books by Julie Yarbrough

A Journey Through Grief
Beyond the Broken Heart
Beyond the Broken Heart Leader Guide
Comfort and Joy
Daily Devotions for Your Grief Journey
Inside the Broken Heart
Present Comfort
Present Comfort Study Edition
Secure in the Storm

GRIEF LIGHT

REFLECTIONS FOR THE HEART

JULIE YARBROUGH

invite
PRESS
Plano, Texas

Then God said, "Let there be light," and there was light.
Genesis 1:3

CONTENTS

HOPE LIGHT

INTRODUCTION

Grief is perhaps the most personal experience in life. At some time, everyone is touched by the pain and sadness of grief. Each experience of death leads us to a different place in life. We can never go back to exactly where we were or who we were before the death of one we love. Our life is never again the same. We are never again the same. Grief changes us for all time.

Over a ten-year period, a kind of cascading grief rolled through my life. The unexpected illness and death of my beloved husband, Leighton Farrell, was my first personal experience of grief. Until then, I had shared in the sadness and grief of others, but never had I occupied a front row seat to dying and death. When my husband died, I was devastated. His death was untimely and tragic. For many months, I was overwhelmed by the loss of his life to mine. Unremitting grief affected my physical, mental, emotional, and spiritual well-being.

Eight months later, my beloved father died. Though his death was not unexpected, when he died, another torrent of large-scale grief washed through my already broken heart. Within a very short period of time, I had lost the two people I loved most in the world.

The fact that my husband and my father died out of order added a layer of emotional confusion to my grief. It was incomprehensible to me that my husband should die before my much older father. At the time, the order of life and death felt existentially unjust.

Eight years later, my mother died. Ours was a complicated, complex relationship. When she died, no amount of self-examination or rationalization could reconcile our fractured relationship in my mind or heart. My grief for her was, in a word, troubled.

This mid-life decade of sequential grief was for me a crisis of body and mind, soul and spirit. Though each experience of grief was different, they were in some ways similar and strangely intertwined. Each grief took me to a new place in life.

Grief Light is a book of reflections written from the heart that offer spiritual insight through illustrations from everyday life—grief lived, grief breathed, grief expressed. Some are practical, some rich in imagery, some illustrate the universal truths of grief, and some are more personal. In each reflection, the grief of my frayed spirit peeks through the fabric of each heartfelt word.

When we grieve, usually it is difficult to focus on much more than a short devotional or a daily thought. If we enjoy a good meal, our digestion thanks us when we take small bites. The reflections in *Grief Light* are small, digestible bites meant to nourish your heart and soul. Each offers direction for spiritual thought with references from scripture for prayer and meditation.

The hope is that the perspective of *Grief Light* is relatable, that as you read these "almost devotionals," you will find yourself thinking, "Oh, yes, that happened to me," or "Now I understand more about what I am feeling," or "I thought I was the only one who had ever experienced that."

Within the darkness of grief, we long for light. We yearn for light even as imperceptibly we move toward the light. My prayer is that the personal heart and spiritual truths of *Grief Light* will help you discover the light of God's love within the darkness of your grief, the light that restores us and makes us whole, the light that leads us into the light of new life.

Julie Yarbrough
Dallas, Texas

SHADOW LIGHT

*Every good and perfect gift is from above, coming down from the
Father of the heavenly lights, who does not change like shifting
shadows.*
James 1:12, 17 NIV

INTO THE WOODS

Most find that grief is a long, winding journey through a vast forest of unfamiliar, often painful emotions. When we grieve, we have no idea where our life is headed or what our life will look like without the one we love. The signposts that point the way through grief are few and far between.

With each journey, I have struggled with direction. In grief, there is no north, south, east or west. There is no reliable compass to help us get our bearings. Our thoughts and feelings are all over the map. We wander and roam; we seek and go astray. We are distracted by the best of our love and the worst of our pain, our senses attuned both to the absence and the presence of the one we love and now grieve. He or she is here, there, and all around us, yet nowhere that we can touch or feel.

If you live in the mountains or have ever visited an ancient forest, perhaps you have a good idea of what it means to be in the woods. I lived in the Black Forest area of Germany for several years. The name perfectly describes how these woods look. The forest is black and dark because of the size, number, and density of its towering, centuries-old trees. The illusion of darkness created by the majesty and beauty of nature is a grief thought to ponder.

Although I am not much of a hiker, I ventured into the Black Forest a few times for some fresh air and exercise. Helen Keller, who was both deaf and blind, wrote, "To me a lush carpet of pine needles or spongy grass is more welcome than the most luxurious Persian rug."[1] In the woods, I found not a lush carpet, but a rough, tangled undergrowth that made for very slow going. As I stumbled along, I had to focus on every step. Because my footing was unsure, I missed the cool pleasure of the forest, its shimmering light filtering through the trees, lingering for a moment in the dust of suspended animation. I missed the enjoyment of the forest because of all those pesky trees.

In truth, I was not properly equipped for a walk in the woods. I did not have the right shoes. If you think about it, grief is the one experience in life for which we cannot prepare. Because we are unprepared for the journey through grief, often we get tripped up—emotionally, spiritually, and yes, even physically in ways we never could imagine.

When we grieve, we have no idea how vast the forest really is. Because we are in the thick of it, all we see is the next tree and then the next. We hold on and hang on for dear life. Can you name the tree that you are clinging to at this moment in your grief? Anger? Fear? Loneliness? Sadness? Worry? Disappointment? Despair? As we grope our way through the dark forest of grief, our pain and heartache block the light of God's comfort and hope. Too easily we forget that light is all around us. The light of God's love is over us, above us, and within us. On our arduous journey through the darkness of grief, God waits until at last we look up and see the bright light that beckons us toward the glade of new life that lies ahead. When we emerge from the forest—tried and tested by our journey through grief—we stand again in the full sunlight of God's love with a grateful heart and hope for the future.

God is light and in him there is no darkness at all.
1 John 1:5

I come from the mountains;
the valley steams, the ocean roars.
I wander, silent and joyless,
and my sighs forever ask: Where?

Here the sun seems so cold,
the blossom faded, life old,
and men's words mere hollow noise;
I am a stranger everywhere.

Where are you, my beloved land?
Sought, dreamt of, yet never known!
The land so green with hope,
the land where my roses bloom,

Where my friends walk,
where my dead ones rise again,
the land that speaks my tongue,
O land, where are you?

I wander, silent and joyless,
and my sighs for ever ask: Where?
In a ghostly whisper the answer comes:
'There, where you are not, is happiness!'[2]

THE JOURNEY

On a lonely Saturday afternoon a few months after my husband died, I went to a movie clad in a self-styled version of sackcloth and ashes. My baggy gray sweat suit felt like a warm cocoon; its hood all but ensured my anonymity. At that moment in my grief, I wanted nothing other than to look like I felt—anonymous and invisible. I headed south into a bag of popcorn, hoping to find some emotional or physical comfort as I ate my way to the bottom. Comfort food—well, we know there is no such thing as that...

As I waited for the previews, an ad for a well-known brand of luggage grabbed my attention. Travel images flashed on the screen accompanied by a thought-provoking message—a journey is not a trip or a vacation. Rather, a journey is both a process and a discovery. As a process of self-discovery, a journey brings us face to face with ourself. On a journey, we see not only the world but also how we fit into the world.

Although I did not rush out to buy the luggage—it would be many months before I was ready to travel again—I thought about the final teaser in the ad. "Does the person create the journey or does the journey create the person?" The message was summed up in less than sixty seconds: "The journey is life itself. Where will life take you?"

Grief is a journey we would rather not take. When one we love dies, suddenly we find ourself on a forced march through strange, unfamiliar, uncharted territory. The journey might well be described as a trek—an arduous slog through the difficulties and challenges of life without the one we love and now grieve. To be sure, generations have grieved before us, others grieve alongside us now, and somewhere the journey of grief begins for someone whose grief is newer than ours.

Whatever our experience of grief, the journey is uniquely our own. No two people ever grieve the same.

There is no map or built-in GPS to show us the most direct route and give us clear directions for our journey through grief. But like all travel, grief begins at some point and ends at some point. When we begin, we have no idea where the journey will lead or how long it will take us to reach our destination. Though we might wish it to be otherwise, there is no back road or easy detour that can take us around grief. There is no shortcut that allows us to bypass or avoid altogether the experience of grief. There are no signposts on the journey that lead us with certainty toward the exit ramp of grief. There is no finish line when we reach the end of our experience with grief. There is no neon sign or billboard that proclaims, "You have arrived," "You are here," or "You've reached your destination." Only you will know when you have completed the journey of grief.

On the way home from work one day, I saw a woman walking outside, striding through the neighborhood with purpose and intent. She was completing her daily exercise circuit, but really, she was not going anywhere except back to her home. When we grieve, our journey is going somewhere. Slowly but surely, the journey of grief leads us away from pain and sorrow toward hope and new life. Over time we learn that there is only one way to make the journey—we walk, as the psalmist writes, "even though I walk" (Psalm 23:4 RSV). We are not asked to jog, run, or race. We walk.

The journey through the valley of the shadow of death is perhaps the longest, most arduous walk of faith we will ever experience in life. The presence of God guides us on our journey and leads us toward spiritual safety and home. We chart our own course and make our own map. Slowly but surely, we make our way through grief in the certainty that God is with us every step of the way, "for you are with me; your rod and your staff, they comfort me" (Psalm 23:4).

....

I walk before the Lord in the land of the living.
Psalm 116:9

....

In the Dark

As I sat in the chair by my bed one night reading a book on solitude and silence, the power went off. The air conditioner whined to a halt, the ceiling fan slowed then stopped, and suddenly, I was in near total darkness. Unlike gradations of light, dark is dark. When there is no light, there is only darkness. The shrill insistence of the security alarm penetrated the darkness. My immediate reaction to whatever real or perceived danger might be lurking in the dark was fight or flight mode. When at last my heart stopped racing, I had a moment of insight—I do not like the dark.

It seemed that my house was the only one in the neighborhood that had no power. I could see light in a nearby house. When the momentary grip of fear eased, I remembered the small flashlight in a nearby drawer, stashed there for just such an emergency. I had no idea whether it would work. Did it need new batteries? Would there be enough light to see so that I could call and report the outage?

I calmed myself, gathered my wits, mastered the flashlight, turned off the security system, and made the call. It was late so I got into bed and waited—no late-night television, no light from a bedside clock, no radio, no light to read a book, no cellphone, no tablet, no computer. I had no idea how long it would take to restore the power, or how long I would be in the dark. Yet I knew with certainty that, at the very latest, there would be light with the dawn of a new day. As I lay there in solitude and silence, I listened intently to the symphony of noise beyond my four walls—insects, birds, cars, and planes—the unsettling sounds of darkness.

When one we love dies, we are powerless to change what happened. Suddenly, unexpectedly, we find ourself alone in the unfamiliar darkness of grief. At its most fundamental, grief is about how we manage our darkness and how we direct light into our life. Though we are never disconnected from the source of our spiritual strength and power, for a while, grief is more about darkness than light. When darkness takes up residence in our soul, God's strength and encouragement extinguish the darkness and light our way toward the light of new life, "May our Lord Jesus Christ himself and God our Father, who loved us and by his grace gave us eternal encouragement and good hope, encourage your hearts and strengthen you in every good deed and word" (2 Thessalonians 2:16–17 NIV).

If you are overwhelmed by emotional or spiritual darkness, you may want to seek the help of a confidential, non-judgmental counselor, qualified professional, therapist, or minister who will listen thoughtfully about your grief. I did. It helps to talk out loud about the personal emotions and challenges of grief. It helps to hear yourself speak what is in your inmost heart. It helps to know that someone who understands is listening and cares. Often God answers our prayer for help by directing us toward one who can guide us away from darkness into light, "If, then, the light in you is darkness, how great is the darkness!" (Matthew 6:23).

Though we live for a while in the dark night of grief, God created light out of great darkness. God is with us in the darkness of our grief. God is light, "God is love" (1 John 4:8 NIV).

·····

*Indeed, you are my lamp, O L*ORD*;*
*the L*ORD *lightens my darkness.*
2 Samuel 22:29

·····

DARKNESS AND LIGHT

Eclipse fever in the United States is over for now. By 3:00 on April 8, festivities were all but over and eclipse glasses were marked down to half price.

Science confirms that there will be a solar eclipse in seven different parts of the world over the next ten years. In the experience-driven culture of the twenty-first century, many people will travel great distances to other countries to see the phenomenon of a total solar eclipse.

Texas was among several states along the path of totality. During the days and weeks of buildup to the event, local media hype was unrelenting. As the date neared, specific information about the time of the eclipse and regular weather updates helped people in the area prepare for a historic moment that, for some, would be a once in a lifetime experience.

Presumably each person poised to see the eclipse had at least a rudimentary understanding of what happens when the moon passes between the earth and the sun, blocking the light of the sun as it passes while casting its shadow on the earth. But seeing the eclipse was different for each person. No two people saw exactly the same thing at exactly the same time. No two photos look the same. During the four minutes of totality, many who observed the eclipse had some private, personal experience, whether intellectual, visceral, or spiritual, whether joy, awe, wonder, or a profound sense of the vast universe set in motion by the God of all creation.

Like so many, I had the requisite safety glasses for viewing the eclipse, but it was a workday, and I had no elaborate plan to celebrate the event. From everything that had been said, both by experts and enthusiasts, I expected the sky to change and become as dark as night before the actual eclipse occurred.

Shortly before the appointed time, I left my office and joined others in the parking lot to share the experience of totality. Perhaps because I live in an urban environment surrounded by ambient light whatever the time of day or night, the sky was not as dark as night. As I looked through the glasses and saw the moon move slowly across the sun, my senses were attuned to the gentle spring breeze wafting through the air and the sun creating a halo to backlight the clouds. In this unexpected moment of awe and reverence, I felt at one with the universe, at one with nature, and at one with God.

In some way, those who witnessed the eclipse experienced this spiritual truth, "the people who walked in darkness have seen a great light; those who lived in a land of deep darkness—on them light has shined" (Isaiah 9:2). Or perhaps we experienced in that moment the other side of this spiritual truth—the people who walk in light have seen a great darkness. The light of God's love guides us through the darkness of grief toward the light of new life, "It is you who light my lamp; the LORD, my God, lights up my darkness" (Psalm 18:28).

He knows what is in the darkness, and light dwells with him.
Daniel 2:22

WHY DO WE GRIEVE?

When one we love dies, most who grieve want answers. Specifically, we want to know the "why?" of death. When my beloved husband died, my greatest need was to understand what happened. I wanted answers to the thousand-and-one questions troubling my soul. To survive and move forward again, I had to make sense of the "how" and "why" of his death.

After several weeks of delving into his medical records and researching the cause and effect of pancreatic cancer, I understood why he died. The clinical answer was clear—he had an aggressive form of terminal disease. But I wanted to know why he got sick. For a seventy-three-year-old man, he was still young—active, full of vitality, and engaged in life. I wanted to know whether he got sick because his body was aging or because of some genetic, hereditary, or biological predisposition to this particular disease. This is the missing piece that I will never know.

Although I sorted out the "why" of his illness, the "why" of grief was another matter entirely. Understanding the scientific became less important as my focus shifted to the larger spiritual question, "Why do we grieve?" At its most fundamental, grief is the outpouring of our human emotions in response to the death of one we love. Though the mind and body are affected by death, the impulse to grieve comes from the depth of our inmost being—our heart, our soul, and our spirit. Grief is the highest expression of God-given love. If we did not love, our heart would not be broken by death. *We grieve because we love.*

Perhaps you are grieving the death of a beloved husband or wife or partner. You may be grieving the untimely, tragic death of a precious child. Perhaps you are grieving the death of a family member or wise parent or someone serving our country. The challenging question of grief is this: would we forego the love we shared with the one now lost to us in death in order to avoid the pain of grief? No, it is unimaginable to think of hedging the joy and glory of love against the pain and heartache of grief. This belies the very nature of love. If we have experienced the breadth and depth of love, when death touches our life, for a while we can do nothing except grieve. Grief suggests a simple ratio: *the more we love, the greater our grief.*

Grief is an expression of the love that endures beyond death. Grief comes from love. Grief springs from love. Grief arises from surrendered, selfless love. Grief is the eternal connection of our love to the one we love and now grieve. Why do we grieve? We grieve because we love.

....

Love knows no limit to its endurance, no end to its trust, no fading of its hope; it can outlast anything. It is, in fact, the one thing that still stands when all else has fallen.
1 Corinthians 13:7–8 PHILLIPS

....

SADNESS

The overarching emotion of grief is a kind of pervasive, relentless sadness. Though sadness is often our first reaction to ordinary loss and disappointment in life, sadness takes on a life of its own when one we love dies. When we grieve, sadness feels like a gaping emptiness in our heart and soul. Sadness feels like the absence of joy and hope in life.

No one can tell us how long we will feel sad because grief is individual and personal. A feeling of sadness may seem inescapable for a few weeks, a few months, or even for several years. Sometimes we allow sadness to become a comfortable habit, which was part of my experience of grief. In my worst moments, I allowed sadness to take me to the edge of depression, but the God of my grief-worn faith kept me from falling into the abyss of deep despair.

One reason we feel sad when we grieve is that we are lonely. We miss our loved one. Death robs us of many of the human joys that fill and complete our life—love, friendship, and the expression of devotion and affection to name only a few. We miss the presence of one with whom we have shared our life. Poet Edna St. Vincent Millay well describes the sadness of grief, "The presence of that absence is everywhere."[3]

We experience sadness in a hundred little things—starting to speak to one who is no longer there, going to bed without saying goodnight, an empty chair at the table, wandering around a too-large house that evokes many of our best and worst memories, giving up our hopes and dreams for the future.

After my husband died, everywhere I looked I saw couples. Some held hands and seemed devoted to each other, as we were; others seemed detached, living parallel yet apart. As I reflected on the complexity of being in relationship with another human being, I wondered why some couples seem only to tolerate each other yet stay together in marriage. I wondered why some couples live together into old age and why, at middle-age, I was alone and bereft. Yet all of my wondering did nothing except feed my sadness. I kept wishing things were as they once were yet knew that they would never again be the same, saddened that my life going forward would not resemble the life that my husband and I had imagined and planned together.

It is a normal part of the experience of grief to feel sadness and sorrow. How could it be otherwise when one we love dies? Yet as we move forward in grief, sadness slowly recedes into the background of our emotional landscape. Other, more positive emotions assume their rightful position at the forefront of our life. When we access the God-given courage and fortitude needed to go on with life, over time we find that sadness is transformed into warm memories of the one we love and now grieve, memories of gratitude for the love we shared and the gifts of love that will be a part of us forever.

Grief teaches us that it is not a betrayal of our loved one to be joyful. As sadness yields to the energy of our God-given human vitality, we are ready to experience joy again in our life. Yet joy requires a certain discipline of spirit, especially in the aftermath of grief, because joy comes from within. Joy is an indescribable gift of God's grace that revives and restores our soul. Because we have known great sadness, we may need to practice joy in order to re-learn what it feels like to experience joy.

Though a whisper of sadness may linger forever in that special place in our heart reserved for the one we love and now grieve, we are alive. It is a mandate of grief that we should live again in fullness of life; it is the promise of God that we will live again in fullness of joy, "Weeping may linger for the night, but joy comes with the morning" (Psalm 30:5).

....

Be merciful to me, Lord, for I am in distress; my eyes grow weak
with sorrow, my soul and body with grief.
Psalm 31:9 NIV

....

How Did We Get Here?

Part of the journey through grief is understanding where we are and how we got here. We want to know what happened that turned our world upside down and landed us in "the valley of the shadow of death" (Psalm 23:4 RSV).

By definition, a valley is a geological depression on the surface of the earth formed over thousands or millions of years. It is the lowest point in a mountain formation. A valley is created when the flow of a river or stream causes natural erosion of the soil and rocks that constitute a mountain or range of hills. A valley follows the course of the river or stream that created it.

The valley of the shadow of death is the lowest point in our grief. When one we love dies, we experience its deep shadows and emotional darkness. The direction and depth of a valley is defined by the river or stream that created it. When we grieve, for a while we lose our sense of direction. We cannot see that the stream leads us away from darkness, out of the shadows toward light and life beyond the valley of the shadow of death.

How did we get here? Some take a free-fall jump off a sheer cliff into the valley with nothing and no one to break the fall. Without so much as a running jump, the sudden illness or unexpected death of a loved one pushes us over the edge with no time to prepare. When my husband was diagnosed with pancreatic cancer and died only ninety days later, I plummeted into the valley. My descent was quick, painful, and not at all graceful. The fall broke every part of my heart, soul, and spirit.

Those who serve as caretakers or caregivers for months or years before the death of a loved one relocate their life and camp out near the valley for the duration of the illness or infirmity. There they live on the edge in constant readiness mode, prepared but never ready to encounter the darkness of the valley. Not unlike the stream that does the work of erosion to create the valley, each day of a prolonged illness is a steady, persistent erosion of life. Those who tend and faithfully care for one who nears death draw nearer to the precipice of the valley with each passing day. Though the inevitability of death is inescapable, those who serve are seldom resigned to the certainty of death. Selfless servants persevere in hope.

Observing the slow, steady demise of my father as he died slowly from the debilitation of Alzheimer's disease was like watching an ice sculpture melt. His once strongly defined physical and mental presence disappeared drop by drop with no hope of salvaging the watery puddle around him. It was impossible to reapply what was lost to make him whole and well again. Even as the disease eroded his mind and body, his heart never forgot the power of love.

It is an unspoken truth that at some time we cry out to God from the depths of our soul when we are bystanders to the slow death of one we love, "How long, LORD, how long?" (Psalm 6:3 NIV). As my father's life came to an end, I struggled against my slow slide into the valley of the shadow of death. I was hanging on to the edge of the cliff for dear life, for his dear life. At the last, I realized that it was the better part of love for me to let go and in so doing, to let him go.

However we get there, when we arrive in the valley, we are surrounded by shadows. Grief is the struggle to overcome the shadows in our life—shadows left over from the past, shadows within the uncertain present, shadows that intimate our unknown future. Yet no shadow exists without light. Within each shadow, the relationship of darkness to light and light to darkness assures us that God, the creator of all light, will overcome the darkness we encounter in the valleys that shadow our lives when we grieve, "in him was life, and the life was the light of all people" (John 1:4).

....

Because of the tender mercy of our God, the dawn from on high will break upon us, to shine upon those who sit in darkness and in the shadow of death, to guide our feet into the way of peace.
Luke 1:78–79

....

How Long Does Grief Last?

Whether you are at the beginning of your experience of grief, near its end, or somewhere in between, often we ask, "How long does grief last?" Though we would like for our grief to be at an end now, this minute, today, it is not humanly possible to control how long grief lasts or when it will be over. More often than not, grief is about complex emotions that defy an orderly progression toward their resolution.

Our technology-driven age insists on instant gratification and quick results. Grief is many things, but it is not an on-demand experience. Nor is it one size fits all. We are powerless to order our experience of grief or dictate its duration and intensity. We cannot turn it off or tune it out with the simple flip of a switch.

There is no pre-ordained, finite, period of time that defines the span of grief. There is no month-to-month chart or daily planner to demonstrate our progress through grief. There is no timetable or set expiration date for grief. Though we would like for grief to be over on a certain date, one that we can circle on our calendar, usually grief lasts longer than we expect.

Social and external pressures to "get over our grief" engender anxiety about how long our grief will last. Rather than a specific timeline, what we really want to know is how long we will feel the pain of grief and when our heartache will subside: "How long must I bear pain in my soul and have sorrow in my heart all day long?" (Psalm 13:2).

Try though we might, we cannot rush or hasten the end of grief. Those who suggest that "by now" we should "be done" with our grief must wait. We cannot schedule our experience of grief for the convenience of those who love us but have little capacity to understand the emotional, physical, and spiritual impact of the death of one we love.

Grief does not come with an instruction book or user's manual that includes a section on how long grief lasts. There is no standard or norm for grief. There are no directions on how long we are supposed to feel what we feel or how long we should grieve. We learn from starts and stops that grief is oblivious to the calendar. How could it be otherwise? There is no way to measure in days, weeks, months, or even years the depth and breadth of our love for the one we now grieve. The answer to "how long does grief last?" is this: We grieve as long as we grieve.

More often than not, grief lasts much longer than we imagine. There is no shortcut around grief or some secret passage that leads us quickly through it. Slowly but surely, we learn that the experience of grief is one of our finest teachers in life. God uses our grief to instruct us in patience and forbearance. God uses our grief to fortify our faith. God uses our grief to inspire strength and courage for life beyond the broken heart.

A young woman whose husband died unexpectedly in a traffic accident on the way to work one day shared with me several months later that she was no longer actively grieving. Her self-knowledge impressed me as remarkably insightful because it had nothing to do with forgetting her husband and the love they shared. Rather, we reach a turning point in our experience of grief when we recognize that gradually we are incorporating the death of our loved one into our life. As we near acceptance, we see that though our experience of grief is now inactive, it will remain part of who we are and who we will become.

How long does grief last? For many, there may be a defining moment such as remarriage that clearly signals the end of grief. For others, it may take several years to work through the deep, lasting emotions of grief.

Seldom is grief at a definitive end once and for all time. We will love and remember the one now lost to us in death always. Though our time of active grief one day nears an end, there will always be a tender shadow that lingers in our spirit and reminds us of the one we love and now grieve. Though life goes on, in a corner of my heart, I will forever grieve the death of my beloved husband.

How long does grief last? Grief lasts as long as it lasts. We grieve as long as we grieve.

Very truly I tell you, you will weep and mourn while the world rejoices. You will grieve, but your grief will turn to joy.
John 16:20 NIV

SEPARATION

The continuum of life that begins with creation is punctuated by separations that begin at birth with our first breath. With a single snip, we are permanently detached from the one who has been our source of physical nourishment for nine months. We are separated from a biological mother who by virtue of her physical ability to give birth is also endowed with a responsibility to shape our understanding of both connection and separation.

While the vast majority of people are born into a maternal relationship of unconditional love that grows and thrives over a lifetime, others are born into a relationship that from the moment of conception is predicated on emotional separation. For an unwanted child, separation can be about rejection by a reluctant parent or being the child of a mother who is incapable or unwilling to love.

Seldom are there do-overs if a child is denied the fundamental, God-given right to be loved. Unless and until a child finds a source of love that is constant, dependable, and reliable—a steady, caring father, a loving grandparent, or a foster or adoptive parent—there is real danger that the child fails to thrive both mentally and emotionally. How we separate at birth determines how we launch into the world. Consider this story of earthly and spiritual separation,

> Now every year his parents went to Jerusalem for the festival of the Passover. And when he was twelve years old, they went up as usual for the festival. When the festival was ended and they started to return, the boy Jesus stayed behind in Jerusalem, but his parents were unaware of this. Assuming that he was in the group of travelers, they went a day's journey. Then they started to look for him

among their relatives and friends. When they did not find him, they returned to Jerusalem to search for him. After three days they found him in the temple, sitting among the teachers, listening to them and asking them questions. And all who heard him were amazed at his understanding and his answers. When his parents saw him they were astonished, and his mother said to him, "Child, why have you treated us like this? Your father and I have been anxiously looking for you." He said to them, "Why were you searching for me? Did you not know that I must be in my Father's house?" But they did not understand what he said to them. Then he went down with them and came to Nazareth and was obedient to them, and his mother treasured all these things in her heart. (Luke 2:41–51)

There was nothing of defiance when Jesus remained in Jerusalem after the festival of the Passover. As an inquisitive, inquiring adolescent, he was where he needed to be to listen and learn more about his Father. The only place that this could happen was in the temple. He assumed that his parents knew where he was. He assumed that they understood who he was. He assumed that they understood his mission in life. After a three-day separation, their reunion was one of relief for his parents. With humility, Jesus accepted his mother's expression of concern and mild admonition for causing them so much anxious worry. Jesus honored his parents with obedience as they returned to Nazareth and resumed their daily routine. His mother cherished her son for as long as he was hers to care for and raise and love unto death. In her heart, she knew that nothing could separate her from Jesus, her earthly son, the only begotten Son of God.

According to author Paul Tripp, "There is often a disconnect between our confessional theology and our street-level functional theology. There is often a separation between the doctrines we say we have embraced and the choices we make and the anxieties we feel."[4] This is especially true when one we love dies. Grief creates a disconnect between what we say we believe and how we act on the emotions triggered by death. Grief nurtures a sense of detachment from our inmost self and often from God. When we create separation and distance between us, God persists. God insists on relationship. The God of all grace never leaves us or forsakes us.

....

I will never leave you or forsake you.
Hebrews 13:5

....

Separated
But Not Lost

At a time when our blended family was intact, my husband and I took everyone to New York City one year to celebrate the Thanksgiving holiday. There were six adults and three children, ranging in age from three to seventy. Though every detail of the trip was carefully planned, inevitably "the best laid plans of mice and men often go awry."[5] And go awry they did.

The long holiday weekend began the night before the traditional parade on Thanksgiving Day. Our first stop was Central Park West at 72nd Street to see the giant character balloons featured in the parade slowly come to life as they were inflated. Knowing that we would be part of a large crowd, our plan was to stay together. But amid the excited throng of children and grown-ups, we were quickly separated. In the panic of the moment, it seemed as though our family members were irretrievably lost for all time.

After a cursory search of the growing crowd, we realized there was little to be done except find our ride and return to the hotel. When we got there, everyone we thought was lost was there—safe, sound, and none the worse for the wear and tear of the adventure. With the matter-of-fact wisdom of a child much older than his years, the five-year-old observed that we had been "separated but not lost in New York City." This expression was quickly adapted as part of our family lore. Through the years it would be used to describe every manner of miscommunication, misdirection, and disconnection that occurred as our family dynamic ebbed and flowed.

Separation is vital for some of the more mundane chores of everyday life. We separate the laundry so that red socks do not turn white clothes pink. We separate our toes for a pedicure so that the polish does not smudge. We style our hair with a part, separating long from short, dark from light. We separate whites from the yolk of an egg and beat them into an omelet or frothy meringue for a pie. Countless gadgets have the sole purpose of separating fat from the meat stock that will be used to create a delicious sauce or gravy served at a holiday meal.

The Bible is full of stories, parables, and examples that describe many of the ways in which we separate ourself from God. Separation can take as many forms as there are human beings, each with different emotions and circumstances that often cause us to feel estranged from God. Within each modality of separation, whether constructive or destructive, involuntary or voluntary, there is unlimited potential for reconciliation with God.

From the story of creation, we learn the power of constructive separation, "And God saw that the light was good, and God separated the light from the darkness" (Genesis 1:4). "And God said, 'Let there be a dome in the midst of the waters, and let it separate the waters from the waters.' So God made the dome and separated the waters that were under the dome from the waters that were above the dome. And it was so. God called the dome Sky" (Genesis 1:6–8). "And God said, 'Let there be lights in the dome of the sky to separate the day from the night, and let them be for signs and for seasons and for days and years, and let them be lights in the dome of the sky to give light upon the earth.' And it was so" (Genesis 1:14–15).

When God breathed life into creation, the world was unblemished, unlimited in its potential for perfect life. We discern the cause and effect of destructive separation in the free will choice made by Adam and Eve. They chose to disregard God's instructions about life in the Garden of Eden. They chose to eat the fruit of the tree of the knowledge of good and evil. Though God warned them of the consequences—if they ate the fruit or even touched it, they would die—they were tempted and could not resist. Because of their decision, life changed forever for all humanity. In doing that which God had forbidden, they willfully separated themselves from God. Despite God's heartbreak and disappointment at their disobedience, God did what God always does. God expressed love and forgiveness.

Involuntary separation may be as subtle, abrupt, or permanent as the end of a relationship, as unequivocal as a final legal decree, or as swift and severe as a cataclysmic event. Often we experience a kind of involuntary spiritual separation from God when we grieve the death of one we love. We feel stunned, bewildered, and confused when one we love dies. We feel separated and lost because our world has been turned on its head by death.

Voluntary separation is a kind of lost and found estrangement during which we wander for a while in a wilderness of our own making before we at last return to God. When we succumb to the distractions and temptations of the world as a consequence of free will choices made in the heat of the moment, our separation from God is voluntary. If we estrange ourself from God, we struggle within ourself until at last we acknowledge the error of our ways and seek restoration to God. The Apostle Paul speaks eloquently about separation from God,

> Who shall separate us from the love of Christ? Shall trouble or hardship or persecution or famine or nakedness or danger or sword? As it is written: "For your sake we face death all day long; we are considered as sheep to be slaughtered." No, in all these things we are more than conquerors through him who loved us. For I am convinced that neither death nor life, neither angels nor demons, neither the present nor the future, nor any powers, neither height nor depth, nor anything else in all creation, will be able to separate us from the love of God that is in Christ Jesus our Lord. (Romans 8:35–39 NIV)

We are assured that neither things present nor things to come will be able to separate us from the love of God. Perhaps we can surmise that the past is included under the catchall, "anything else in all creation."

The reality of our human experience, especially when we grieve, is that the past can affect our relationship with God. If our life has been shaped by a loveless upbringing, an abusive marriage, a failed relationship, or any other iteration of emotional damage, misuse, or rejection, the past is fraught with issues of emotional trust that affect how we relate to God and to others.

When death occurs, we do not lose someone we love, only his or her physical presence. Nothing of that person is lost except a mortal body. The heart and soul of the one we love and grieve lives on in eternity. Though we are separated, we are never lost. Neither death nor life can separate us from the love of God. Nothing can; nothing ever will.

Blessed be the Lord, *for he has wondrously shown his steadfast love to me when I was beset as a city under siege. I had said in my alarm, "I am driven far from your sight." But you heard my supplications when I cried out to you for help.*
Psalm 31:21–22

ESTRANGEMENT

Whatever our faith conviction or lack thereof or our complete indifference to the power and presence of the Almighty, it is impossible to estrange ourself from God. God is the creator of the universe, the giver of life to every child of God's creation, the inexhaustible source of love in this world and beyond.

We may turn our back on God, but God never turns away from us, "Where can I go from your spirit? Or where can I flee from your presence? If I ascend to heaven, you are there; if I make my bed in Sheol, you are there" (Psalm 139:7–8). Since the beginning of creation, the faith of humankind in the power and presence of God has been tried and tested. Whatever our separation, no estrangement is hopeless.

If we pay attention, we see people every day who are homeless. Each is a beloved child of God; each is a reflection of the image of God, "So God created humans in his image, in the image of God he created them" (Genesis 1:27). Whatever the reason, cause, or circumstance, those who live within the parameters and structure of society yet struggle to meet their basic human needs each day know the reality of estrangement.

There is a small median at the intersection of a neighborhood street and a major highway that I pass by almost every day on the way to work. The scruffy, neglected patch has a sad, unkempt tree and a tenacious cactus snarled with trash, leaves, and debris. On this small wasteland at an important corner, homeless people stand with signs that ask for help. One day, I noticed a man whose message tugged at my heart.

His sign said that he was homeless because he had been in prison. His sign said that he was looking for work. I drove through the intersection but made a U-turn at the first opportunity. I went around the block and returned to the intersection to respond to his apparent need for help. Through the car window, I handed him a bill. To my surprise, he reached into his backpack and gave me a neatly folded piece of paper. He asked me to read it when I had time. When I got to the office, I unfolded the letter and read this message, written on lined paper in neat penmanship:

> I would like to say I appreciate whatever gesture you gave me even if the gesture was only a smile. I have nothing to smile about until someone smiles at me first and then I smile because the only response to a smile is a smile. When someone laughs at you it may create a frown or a confused blank expression but a smile creates a smile every time. Try it!!
>
> Some people will never support you because they're afraid of what you may become. I can't tell you the key to success. But the key to failure is trying to please everybody. I matured off pain not age. If the goal sets you apart from the crowd, stay alone. Being alone for a while is dangerous. It's addicting once you see how peaceful it is. You don't want to deal with people anymore. When you learn to survive alone, you survive everything.
>
> A hungry stomach, an empty pocket and a broken heart can teach the best lessons of life. Pain changes people. It makes you trust less, overthink more, and shut people out. Pain will leave once it has finished teaching you. I don't regret the things I've done. I regret the things I never had the chance to do. Some people measure time in seconds, minutes, days, and even years. I measure time by missing my daughter.

I knew there would not be enough time at this light for me to properly 'thank you' so I wrote this to thank you. It's easy to forget someone who says 'thank you' but hard to forget a written 'thank you'.

Respectfully, Eric

We live our days in pursuit of a self-determined life. We see ourself as independent, self-reliant, and capable—until we are not. At some time, whether by outward force or personal circumstance, we are reduced to a state of helplessness. Too often we turn to God only as a last resort. When one we love dies, grief distorts our sense of place in the world. The estrangement of grief brings us to our knees

When we separate ourself from God, God does not weaponize love and use it against us. Love is the essence of God. The love of God is not self-serving, nor does it seek to possess or control. The love of God never hesitates or falters. It is constant, steadfast, and unconditional. Because God loves us, God is for us. There is no estrangement in all of creation that can separate us from the love of God.

In this is love, not that we loved God but that he loved us.
1 John 4:10

EMPTY GRIEF

When my mother died, my grief might best be described as disorienting. Though her death did not come as a shock or a surprise, in the aftermath of her death, I felt strangely upended. When the circle of life at last comes to a close, for those who survive, grief may feel somehow defective or incomplete because of the ragged edges and gaping holes in a relationship.

Through long months of slow, grinding decline, I was no more than a helpless onlooker, watching and waiting until at last her life yielded to death. As I kept the final vigil by her bedside, I realized that I had lived a large chunk of my life on call, waiting to spring into action for the next crisis or emergency. In the end, there was nothing more I could do other than to be present. Though our relationship was complicated and complex, damaged and bruised, love was the only thing I could bring to her dying body and spirit.

What many experience is that bedside time is a chronos world away from life beyond the four walls of a room. Though the minutes tick by, those who sit and wait in high tension and exhausted expectation are in a surreal place of time and space that has little to do with the rest of the world. As slowly death neared, I felt a deep longing to reconnect to the life and to the world at a safe place somewhere, anywhere beyond the reality of imminent death.

As I sat waiting, I found myself lost in random, short-circuit thoughts. They were troubling and deep. They were about my mother. In my head, I heard the recital of our life's history together. The internal monologue began with my childhood and leafed through every chapter of our fractured relationship. Somewhere in my mind, I was attempting to rewrite our personal narrative. Though I connected the dots of our past, the outcome was always the same. I hurt for what was not and for what had never been, heavy thoughts left me wounded and in pain. In the end, I could do nothing other than release our imperfect past to the understanding and grace of God and leave it there.

As I struggled to untangle the complex emotions at the heart of a knotty grief, I felt an overwhelming emptiness. It is not wrong to feel empty when we are drained by a protracted experience of illness and death. Objectively, I was able to attribute at least some of the void to sheer physical exhaustion. Yet not every grief is from a heart broken by love. In some relationships, heartbreak stems from what the mind says should have been our reality, but the heart knows was not.

Space and time improve our perspective. When one we love dies and a relationship is in pieces, inevitably we experience a degree of emotional confusion. It is a duty of grief to care for ourself, to attend to our mental and physical needs as an important first step toward personal recovery. "O Lord, by these things people live, and in all these is the life of my spirit. Oh, restore me to health and make me live!" (Isaiah 38:16).

The power and presence of God soothes our spirit, calms our soul, and satisfies the emptiness within our heart through every experience of relationship, life, death, and grief. God is present to us through the dark night of death. God is faithful. God is with us. Always.

For the Lord has comforted his people
and will have compassion on his suffering ones.
Isaiah 49:13

FEAR IN GRIEF

When we grieve, fear is insidious. It lurks around every corner, waiting to pounce with a full-frontal assault on our wounded heart. When fear strikes, we feel its vise-like grip squeeze our heart. We tremble from the inside out, susceptible to anything and everything that compounds our fear and threatens to make it real.

Death leaves us vulnerable to fear. When one we love dies, fear pushes us to the edge of our mental and emotional capacity, we are shaken to the core of our being. It is not unusual to experience a kind of rampant, all-consuming fear when we grieve, at least for a while.

Why does grief incite our fear? For most, grief is strange new territory; the emotions we feel are foreign and unfamiliar. Often we fear the emotions of grief as much as anything else. At the best of times, it is work to stay in touch with our emotions. When one we love dies, it takes an almost superhuman effort to sort through our emotions and own our feelings about death, our loved one, and ourself. We may be afraid of what we will discover if we look within and examine our heart.

The experience of grief is often characterized by a series of emotional interludes. At different times, in different ways, the emotions of grief demand our attention. When we grieve, we live through interludes of fear and uncertainty. During these interludes, it is not unusual to feel detached, isolated, and indifferent to life in general and, more particularly, to our own life. Without our loved one, we are fearful. We do not know who we are, where we are, or where we are going.

To be sure, fear is a very real part of grief. We do not imagine fear or conjure it up. When we grieve, fear can take on a life of its own. Writer, scholar, and theologian C.S. Lewis wrote, "No one ever told me that grief felt so like fear."[6] Fear enters into our lives in unexpected ways. Fear sets off a turf war within our soul, a conflict that rages for a while between what we feel and what we believe. Grief is the battleground of our heart, mind, soul, and spirit. Fear strikes at the heart of all we believe. Fear tests the substance and depth of our faith. We bear witness to our faith as we struggle and at last conquer our grief-born fear.

Fear feeds on the shock of grief. A few days after my husband died, I was overwhelmed by shock. His death seemed unreal to me—how could it be? In that moment, I came face to face with the reality of grief as cold fear washed through my entire being—the daily, relentless kind of fear that is irrational yet very real. Yet through it all, fear could not move the conviction of my faith, "Many will see and fear and put their trust in the LORD" (Psalm 40:3). From time to time, Leighton preached on Psalm 23. I had no idea what it meant to go through "the valley of the shadow of death" until I stood at its edge waiting for the moment of his death. When he died, I plunged headfirst into the valley of the shadow of death. What greeted me in the depths of the valley was my raging, unfaithful fear. For a while, my life seemed on a collision course with the vast, frightening unknown. I lived in fear every day. I had no idea whether or not I would survive. It would be many months before I understood the "fear no evil" admonition of the psalmist about death and grief.

In my head, I knew that my fear was disproportionate to the reality and circumstance of my everyday life. My towels were beginning to fray, but I feared spending the money to buy new ones. I agonized over whether I could afford to keep our home. Two days after the funeral, the iron broke. Buying a new one was a daunting task that felt one size too large for my grief. It rained, the roof leaked, and all I knew to do was to get out the buckets and watch them fill. At the time, life seemed to be defined by a series of small disasters that to me seemed nothing short of catastrophic. Fear was attached to every small and large thing that happened.

Fear is a normal part of grief. When we grieve, for a while it may seem impossible to do anything other than give in to our fear. This is a normal part of our human response to the death of one we love. We turn a corner in understanding the emotions that are driving our grief when we acknowledge that fear is our first reaction to the death of one we love.

Fear feeds on physical and mental shock until that time when the dense fog of shock begins to lift. As we become more rested and present to ourself, we move beyond the initial shock of death and enter more fully into the experience of grief. When we understand the cause and effect of our fear, we marshal our spiritual resources—prayer, faith, and hope—to disempower every fear. God is faithful on our journey through the valley of the shadow of death. We fear no evil because God is with us.

For I, the LORD your God, hold your right hand; it is I who say to you, "Do not fear, I will help you."
Isaiah 41:13

FEAR-FUL

When we grieve, fear crowds our hearts and minds. There, it finds space to grow and thrive. It takes very little to put us into an emotional tailspin that spirals downward to a deep, dark place of fear where we learn what it feels like to be full of fear, fear-ful. According to statesman and philosopher Edmund Burke, "No passion so effectually robs the mind of all its powers of acting and reasoning as fear."[7]

Fear has the power to immobilize us when we grieve. Fear paralyzes our ability to make decisions. Fear causes us to question every action and reaction, large and small. We experience fear in many different forms. Anxiety, worry, dread, agitation, apprehension, alarm, and panic are many of the ways we express our fear when one we love dies.

In grief, we are affected by everything that challenges our competency and our faith. It is not unusual to feel helpless, powerless, and hopeless for a while. Death creates an empty space in our life, a kind of emotional vacuum easily filled by an array of dire thoughts and negative suggestions that nurture our fear. What causes us to be so fearful?

- We fear the present. When one we love dies, suddenly we are forced to take a look at our own life. Many are fearful about the possibility of becoming ill, having an accident, or dying.

- We fear change. When one we love dies, everything changes, nothing stays the same. Our lives will never be the same again.

- We fear the unknown. What will happen in the future? How will life go on? Do I have enough money? Where will I live? Who will take care of me?

- We fear the future. We use valuable emotional energy when we spend time being fearful about what life might hold for us in the immediate or distant future. No one knows what will happen five years, five months, five days, five hours, five minutes, or even five seconds from now.

We take the first step toward dismantling our fear when we acknowledge to God and to ourself that we are fearful. We name what we feel: we are afraid. If we recognize fear for what it is, we can do something about it. We confront our fear, dismantle it, and move forward in faith. Fear is a compelling force when we grieve. From time to time, we will experience again the familiar, cold chill of fear. When we recognize fear, we attribute it to our grief and manage it. We dismiss it as baseless and of the moment. Along the way, we discover that through the grace of God, we have within us the strength and power to conquer our worst fears.

More often than not, fear is our first reflex emotion when one we love dies. Yet fear does not have the power to define our life. In moments when we are awash in fear, we breathe—in and out—until we are no longer filled with fear—fear-ful. As we inhale and exhale, we allow the fresh air of the Holy Spirit through the presence of God to fill our heart, our mind, our soul, and our spirit with the life-giving breath of God's perfect peace, "The LORD is my light and my salvation; whom shall I fear? The LORD is the stronghold of my life; of whom shall I be afraid?" (Psalm 27:1).

....

I sought the LORD, and he answered me
and delivered me from all my fears.
Psalm 34:4

....

FEAR-LESS

We are created to be fear-less, "For God has not given us a spirit of fear, but of power and of love and of a sound mind" (2 Timothy 1:7 NKJV). From birth, we are programmed to resist fear because we are endowed with the best of all that is from God—power, love, and a sound mind. What is it, then, about grief that allows fear to overwhelm our spirit?

One of the most persistent, daily ways in which we express fear is worry. For many, worry is a comfortable, lifelong habit. We worry about the present, the future, and everything in between. Grief distorts our fear. Grief exaggerates our impulse to worry. A spark of fear can become a bonfire of worry when the unknown overpowers us, especially when one we love dies.

One of the qualities I loved most about my husband is that he seldom worried. He lived the truth of his beliefs, "And which of you by worrying can add a single hour to your span of life?" (Matthew 6:27). At the onset of his illness, Leighton spent many days at home in bed. During those long hours, without discernible fear or worry, he reflected on his life and contemplated his impending death. Once asked to summarize his faith, without a moment's hesitation, he replied, "God's grace is sufficient." As he declined in health, he held fast to this unshakeable conviction, "My grace is sufficient for you, for power is made perfect in weakness" (2 Corinthians 12:9).

We talked about fear. He accepted the prognosis that he would soon die. He was unafraid to the end. In marked contrast to his fearless calm, I descended into the dark abyss of fear. I feared for Leighton. I feared for myself. Worry became what felt like a full-time occupation. I worried about what seemed like every possible worst-case scenario. Yet through it all, I was driven by the naïve belief that if I tried hard enough, the force of my love could save him. For many weeks, I hid my fear behind a bright facade of lip-service encouragement and empty hope.

I resisted the chaos caused by his illness with every fiber of my being. I felt as though I was at war within myself, fighting a losing battle with the reality of unalterable change. Going home each night to an empty house after long hospital days was disconcerting. I was alone. I sensed that our world was ending, yet I was powerless to stop it. Fear and worry are the fallout of forced adjustment and change.

As Leighton and I prayed together during the eight weeks of his hospitalization, I felt like a spiritual amateur, a faith fraud who spoke strength and courage, yet lived each day somewhere between hope and despair. Imperceptibly our roles began to shift. As his healthcare advocate, I became the not-so-fearless leader. With the grace of a noble soul, he relied on my strength and support. He was visibly relieved when at last he let go and entrusted decisions about his life and death to my judgment. The responsibility for his life triggered my worst fears. I could pray little more than "Lord, help me" (Matthew 15:25).

Seldom did Leighton ask others to pray for him. When he did, the prayer he requested was for calmness of spirit. As his life ended, there was a perfect calm about his spirit because every matter of the soul and spirit was perfectly resolved in his relationship with God. As a man of great faith, he was fear-less. He died as he lived, without fear.

Grief is an exposé of the extremes of our human emotions. When one we love dies, it is not uncommon to experience within our soul a conflict between fear and faith. We overcome fear through the power of faith and live into the future with fear-less hope, "I believe that I shall see the goodness of the LORD in the land of the living. Wait for the LORD; be strong, and let your heart take courage; wait for the LORD!" (Psalm 27:13–14).

Out of my distress I called on the LORD; the LORD answered me and set me free. With the LORD on my side I do not fear.
What can man do to me?
Psalm 118:5–6 RSV

LIFE LIGHT

I love the LORD because he has heard my voice and my supplications. Because he inclined his ear to me, therefore I will call on him as long as I live. The snares of death encompassed me...I suffered distress and anguish. Then I called on the name of the LORD, "O LORD, I pray, save my life!"
Psalm 116:1–4

ANXIOUS ABOUT
EVERYTHING

The summer that my mother died, I tackled the daunting task of cleaning out the house that my parents had lived in for over twenty-five years. I am not one to procrastinate, but I realized before I began that I was anxious about making a start. I felt dread, sadness, and a strange foreboding about the magnitude of the project ahead. Would I be able to sort it all out and make appropriate dispositions? Would I be a good steward? I wondered, too, whether I had the physical stamina and energy it would take to complete the job. In my inmost heart, I knew that part of my reluctance was selfish. I did not want to sacrifice a month of my life on the altar of their stuff. But the job had to be done, and I chose to do it sooner rather than later.

At some point, most who grieve succumb to some form of anxiety. For some, it is a mild fear of uncertainty; for others, it is more severe, expressed as self-doubt and chronic worry. For those who worry about everything large and small, sometimes to the point of agonizing, anxiety may become a lifestyle.

If we are unable to cope with the circumstances of life because of real or imagined fear, anxiety can cause both emotional and physical distress. When we grieve, often we struggle to release our grip on fear and trust that God is present to us, individually and personally. "Humble yourself, therefore, under God's mighty hand, that he may lift you up in due time. Cast all your anxiety on him because he cares for you" (1 Peter 5:6–7 NIV).

The anxiety of grief is expressed in many ways. When a parent dies, children, especially young ones, are anxious about who is in charge. They want to know who will be there to love them and provide for their needs. When a child dies, parents are anxious about their other children, those they cherish all the more for their loss. They hold them close and pray for their future all the more fervently. When a beloved husband or wife dies, the surviving spouse is anxious about the support structure of his or her daily life—who will provide and care for them, who will be there for companionship, love, and friendship.

God gives us specific instructions on how to manage our anxiety, "Do not be anxious about anything, but in everything by prayer and supplication with thanksgiving let your requests be made known to God" (Philippians 4:6). First, we are instructed not to be anxious about anything. When we grieve, often this is a tall order. Second, we are to pray about everything. Not just the big things but everything, large and small. If we pay attention in life, we see that God cares about the details of our life, that nothing is insignificant to God. Finally, we are to ask God to meet our needs in a spirit thankfulness. We express our gratitude to God in advance, in the certain belief that God is at work in our life in ways unknown and unseen to us. God listens, God hears our prayers, God answers our prayers. We learn from the experience of grief that God's timing is not always our timing and that God's answer is not always the answer we desire, but God's answer is always the voice of love.

We are not anxious because God is present to us always, "Don't worry about anything; instead, pray about everything. Tell God what you need, and thank him for all he has done" (Philippians 4:6 NLT).

....

Don't fret or worry. Instead of worrying, pray. Let petitions and praises shape your worries into prayers, letting God know your concerns. Before you know it, a sense of God's wholeness, everything coming together for good, will come and settle you down. It's wonderful what happens when Christ displaces worry at the center of your life.
Philippians 4:6–7 MSG

....

THIS SIDE OF GRIEF

G rief has the power to create divides in our life, sometimes deep chasms. Often it feels as though it is "us" and
"them"—those who understand and know what it is to
grieve and those who have not yet come face to face with the pain
and heartbreak of death.

Not unlike the Continental Divide, when we grieve there is an
invisible line that separates us from others. Those who do not know
what it feels like to grieve shower us with well-intentioned words
meant to comfort us in our grief. Yet many expressions of sympathy
somehow seem to diminish the death of one we love—the casual
sentiment of a condolence card, an impersonal sympathy note, an
insensitive comment spoken in haste. Many well-worn bromides offered for our comfort often serve only to compound our grief.

No one who is grieving wants to hear expressions intended as
condolence that discount the death of one we love, "At least he is not
in pain anymore," "She is at rest now," "It is for the best," "There is
a reason for everything." More often than not, ready-made comfort
clichés intensify our pain because they deny our loss. Mindless, impersonal expressions of condolence generally do little except add to
the pain in our heart.

Eight short months after my husband died from pancreatic cancer,
my father died of Alzheimer's disease. Piled onto to the profound grief
caused by my husband's death, the grief of my beloved father's death
left me reeling. The effect of compound grief pushed me to the edge of
my emotional capacity for pain. I was in every way heartbroken.

At a small reception following the memorial service for my father, an acquaintance, who just happened to be a clergy spouse, seemed to think that it was her mission to set me straight about grief. She got within inches of my face and began quoting scripture, all the while lecturing me on how I should just.… Well, I don't remember what she actually said, except that her ill-chosen words that day somehow were supposed to make short work of my grief. What I do recall is my visceral reaction to her verbal assault. My first impulse was to lash out physically in response to her clumsy, heartless insensitivity. Instead, I turned around and simply walked away. She was clueless. Though she had been a spectator to the grief of others, not until years later when her husband died did she experience my side of grief.

Despite the insult and injury inflicted on those who grieve by the thoughtless words of others, forgiveness takes us to a different place in grief, "He who forgives an offense seeks love, but he who repeats a matter alienates a friend" (Proverbs 17:9 RSV). These words of wisdom well describe the value proposition of the "forgive and forget" dilemma of grief. When we hang onto inept words that wound and hurt us or harbor resentment toward those who say or do the wrong thing, we are the ones who suffer. Though it may seem counterintuitive, the best response of our heart is to forgive. When we forgive, we feel relief almost immediately. When we forgive, somehow our grief feels lighter, less weighty, and a little more manageable, at least in the moment.

Over a lifetime, we learn the value and blessing of forgiveness. What we find, though, is that forgetting is easier said than done. When our heart is broken by the death of one we love, we remember the time in our life when we were most vulnerable and wounded. For some, that time may be now. I still duck and run when I see the woman who accosted me, but I do not waste valuable emotional energy remembering or reliving that particular moment in my grief. When we forgive and forget, we take an important step toward spiritual recovery from grief.

This side of grief will forever be a part of who we are. Here we live apart from the world for a while in a private place that instructs our heart. Here we learn more about our God-given strength, resilience, and capacity for steadfast endurance. This side of grief teaches us more about who we are. This side of grief shows us who we are becoming. This side of grief is an experience of faith like no other. This side of grief instructs us in hope, "Why are you cast down, O my soul, and why are you disquieted within me? Hope in God, for I shall again praise him, my help and my God" (Psalm 42:11).

....

I consider that the sufferings of this present time are not worth
comparing with the glory about to be revealed to us.
Romans 8:18

....

GRIEF SPEAK

Over the past few years, I have experienced the death of my closest family members—my husband, my father, and my mother. Though I do not profess to be an expert on the subject, I have probably heard most of the expressions of sympathy that constitute the language of grief speak. The downside of grief speak is that more often than not, the trite remarks offered in the name of comfort hurt more than they help.

The story of the death of David's beloved child is a biblical paradigm for the power of sensitive, yet honest grief speak, "But when David saw that his servants were whispering together, he perceived that the child was dead, and David said to his servants, 'Is the child dead?' They said, 'He is dead'" (2 Samuel 12:19). Perhaps it is worth noting that David's servants did not say that his son had "passed away," a euphemism often used to avoid the reality of death. The story ends with David's declaration of faith, "But now he is dead... Can I bring him back again? I shall go to him, but he will not return to me" (2 Samuel 12:23). In a compelling testimony to his faith, David did not mince words or waste his emotional capital on empty grief speak.

Often those who grieve feel resentful when someone presumes that they know what you are feeling. In grief speak moments when would-be comforters have said, "I understand" or "I know how you feel," I have struggled with my better self and resisted the impulse to disavow their assumption. How could they know how I feel? It is not humanly possible to understand or know what another is feeling, no matter how similar the experience of death and grief.

We are subjected to another well-worn expression of grief speak when others refer to the death of our loved one as a "blessing." A third-party pronouncement that the death of our loved one is a "blessing" usually does little to comfort us or ease our grief. I have asked myself on more than one occasion exactly who is blessed when one we love dies. If our loved were alive and able to respond, likely he or she would not think of death as a blessing, no matter how dire the medical circumstances or certainty of death might be. Blessing and death are seldom synonymous in the vocabulary of grief speak.

"Relief" is a sticky word that creeps into the sly inuendo of grief speak. When we do something for someone in the name of compassion, for however long our self-giving may last, relief is never the outcome. Relief is when the pain of a stubborn headache or toothache or backache goes away. Relief is when the heat of summer finally cools to autumn. Relief is when the diagnosis is not cancer or some other life-threatening disease. Relief is when we know our loved ones are safe after a catastrophic weather event or storm.

When my mother died, several of her friends suggested in notes and emails that I should feel relieved. Though my mother was sick for several years and at times her care was all-consuming, not for a moment since her death has my feeling been one of relief. Seeing her through to the end of her life was a life-or-death responsibility. Though I felt drained and exhausted when she died, rather than relief, I felt gratitude that I had the means and the ability to do the hard job of caring for someone who rejected my leadership and love at every turn. Did I do it perfectly? No, surely not. But when we persevere and do all that we can to get it right, in the end, there is no guilt and little regret. When we try and do our utmost, the unexpected reward for our tenacity and perseverance is not relief but a pervasive sense of God's peace.

Seldom are we comforted by the superficial platitudes of grief speak that are tossed our way in the name of condolence and sympathy:

- The "at least" suggestions that do little to meet us at our place of sorrow: "He is not suffering anymore," "She is in a better place."
- The presumptions that trivialize our grief: "It is for the best," "She is better off," "God just needed another angel."

The choice of words that differentiates grief speak from authentic expressions of empathy and compassion is rooted in our fundamental human aversion to death. If we have no reference for personal grief, generally we are uncomfortable with the grief of others. We want those who grieve to be "over it"—quickly. We expect them to "move on with their life"—today. Grief speak abounds in urgency and impatience. When we grieve, we soon learn that the desire of others cannot affect or shorten the duration of our grief.

The idioms of grief speak are of little use to those who seek to live in spiritual solidarity with those who grieve. If we attempt to imagine and live into the pain of another before we make a call or write a note, likely our expression of heartfelt condolence will be words that comfort and bless rather than grief speak. When we begin with "you" and "your" rather than "I," we become care givers and heart menders who ask in love, "How are you feeling in your heart?" When we listen, we hear God speak words of comfort wrapped in the understanding of human compassion. The voice of God transcends every expression of grief speak.

....

Let the words of my mouth and the meditation of my heart be
acceptable to you, O Lord, my rock and my redeemer.
Psalm 19:14

....

FACE FIRST

I n the build-up to a significant remembrance day, I felt the familiar rumbling of memories that evoked sadness and joy, longing and gratitude, and grief refreshed and renewed. It could not be otherwise when a great love is distant yet ever present and always near.

As I walked toward a favorite lunch counter that day, distracted by dark shadows of remembrance, I tripped over a carpet strip that served as the transition from a soft surface to a large expanse of marble flooring. For a nanosecond, I felt myself airborne, my body arced to land with a graceless thud. I have tripped and fallen at other times but never so inelegantly. As I lay sprawled face first on the hard marble, somewhere in my head I heard my beloved father say, "pick up your feet."

Though I was oblivious to the curiosity of dispassionate onlookers, as is so often the case, there were angels around me, people whose first impulse is always to care about others. The lunch counter man left his customers and rushed to help. Two sales associates from the nearby fragrance department saw my distress and offered their assistance and comfort.

I was well and truly shaken, both inside and out. Surely I looked to all the world like a limp rag doll. In that moment, the pent-up emotions of the day collided with the indignity of my bruised body and wounded vanity. I could do nothing other than sit there, legs splayed, and allow my tears to flow.

With the help of two strong men, I made it to my feet, dusted myself off, and assured those who had gathered to help that I would be all right. Without self-pity or drama, I limped to the lunch counter, dazed and still snuffling. Each step suggested that my right ankle, elbow, and shoulder had absorbed the brunt of the blow. As I took a seat and assessed the damage to my chin, upper lip, and knees, the counter man discreetly gave me a bag of ice wrapped in a napkin to put wherever it hurt. When I finished my lunch and thanked him again for his kindness, he murmured words of assurance meant to restore my self-confidence. He seemed adept at knowing just the right thing to say and do. Clearly God used him that day as an agent of care for me—body, heart, and soul. Though I was sore for several days, nothing was broken other than my spirit.

There is no finer gift from grief than the kind of spiritual growth that makes us struggle and question—circumstances, emotions, and yes, even God. Spiritual growth leads us to new, unexpected places in our understanding of both life and death. Spiritual growth allows us to appreciate the truth of scripture in new ways.

Though a fall seemed too much to bear on a day already fraught with the pain of loving remembrance, within the moment, there was an impetus for spiritual growth. The psalmist David wrote with an undertone of warning and an overtone of gratitude from long years of experience with adversity and the challenges of life, "Our steps are made firm by the LORD when he delights in our way; though we stumble, we shall not fall headlong, for the LORD holds us by the hand" (Psalm 37:23–24).

Until my recent face-plant, I had always considered the more literal meaning of this scripture. In truth, I felt a little let down by God when I not only stumbled but also fell headlong. But this is not right thinking. These words are not about our health and well-being but about how we follow God's direction and God's faithful, steadfast presence in our life.

Since the death of my husband, I have come to rely on God's hand holding mine, "Nevertheless, I am continually with you; you hold my right hand" (Psalm 73:23). When I fell, it was as though for an instant God had let go of my hand. In truth, I think this is what upset me the most about the fall that day.

Within the assurance that God is always present to us, there is no promise that nothing will ever go wrong in our life. When our heart aches because of the death of one we love, the promise that overcomes every adversity is that God is with us always, holding our hand, "If I take the wings of the morning and settle at the farthest limits of the sea, even there your hand shall lead me, and your right hand shall hold me fast" (Psalm 139:9–10). God is faithful. God is with us, even when we fall face first.

For you have delivered my soul from death and my feet from falling, so that I may walk before God in the light of life.
Psalm 56:13

WISDOM AND INSIGHT

For each of the three times that I have done the business of estate settlement, I have called on two old friends that have sustained me through many days of difficult decision-making: wisdom and insight. I remember sitting at the desk in my office a few days after my husband died, gathering my wits so that I could focus on what needed to be done. Leighton and I had discussed his business and mine on several occasions. In theory, I understood his estate. In truth, I had little first-hand knowledge of the details of his business because we had managed separately, though never in secret. When he died, I felt unsure, filled with self-doubt, second-guessing every decision.

When one we love dies, for some it is the first time in life that it has been necessary to manage, cope, and deal with the practicalities of daily living. In the days and weeks following the death of one we love, most who grieve experience brain fog, which is caused most often by shock. Symptoms of brain fog include forgetfulness, inability to focus or concentrate, and a limited attention span. The temporary brain fog of grief is one way nature protects us from being overwhelmed by sorrow. When my husband died, I knew nothing about the physical manifestations of grief. I wondered what was wrong with my mind, why I felt so remote, so out of touch with myself. I could not shake the feeling of being an observer to my own life. For a while, grief felt very much like an out of body experience.

Try though I might, the force of my will could not power through the fog that shrouded my brain. For a while, shock seemed to be a persistent condition. I was forced to slow down until one day the fog slowly began to lift. As a mental and economic safety precaution, I realized that I would need to do business in slow motion, at least for a while. Though it felt counterintuitive, I worked at a kind of mental half speed until I began to think more clearly.

As I struggled to work and make sense of the business of life, intuitively I knew that I needed help much larger than any panacea, pill, or professional. I needed the guidance that only God could provide. I began to pray about my feelings of inadequacy and my uncertainty about what to do. Specifically, I asked God for wisdom and insight. Every day my prayer was the same. I did not want to make stupid or costly mistakes. I did not want to be hasty or precipitant and set myself up for regret later on. I was committed to getting the business of our life right, for my sake and for Leighton's sake. I heard his voice in my head saying, "stay calm, it will all work out." This gave me comfort, even as God faithfully answered my persistent, often desperate prayer.

When we pray for wisdom and insight, God directs our thoughts and actions, often in unexpected ways, "Turn your ear toward wisdom, and stretch your mind toward understanding. Call out for insight, and cry aloud for understanding" (Proverbs 2:2–3 CEB). Sometimes God's wisdom comes to us as courage to ask for help, to ask for leniency, or even the forgiveness of a debt. When we pray for insight, God clears our mind of fear and distraction so that we can think rationally, reason objectively, and make wise decisions, "live, and walk in the way of insight" (Proverbs 9:6).

The better part of wisdom may be a thoughtful pause. The better part of wisdom may be deferring an action, a signature, or something final until we are beyond the initial shock of grief and thinking with more than just a broken heart. Over time, we recover our ability to think clearly and make wise decisions. When we see that we are capable of managing whatever tasks and challenges arise, we celebrate each small victory.

We are assured that God answers the prayers of our heart when we pray for wisdom and insight. We are assured that God answers the prayers of our deep, personal, everyday needs, especially when we grieve, "With all wisdom and insight he has made known to us the mystery of his will" (Ephesians 1:8–9).

....

The Lord gives wisdom;
from his mouth come knowledge and understanding.
Proverbs 2:6 CEB

....

RIDING BACKWARD

On the way to work one morning, I decided to drive an extra block east to avoid the off-ramp congestion of the freeway. I ended up on a street that always evokes fond memories of my father. After he retired, his office, once a fixture on this well-travelled street, was sold and torn down to make way for urban improvements. Now the tracks for the area rapid transit system bisect this route to my office. That day, the signal lights flashed, and the crossing arm went down.

I stopped and waited for the commuter train to pass. As I sat idling in my car, passengers on the train caught my attention, especially the ones riding backward. The view for those who ride backward is what those who face forward have already seen. Though the landscape is the same, the backward-facing view looks somehow different—perhaps it is an illusion of angle or perhaps the perspective of light. Those riding backward cannot see what lies ahead until it has passed them by.

When we grieve, for a while we are the ones riding backward. We understand the view because we are familiar with what lies behind us. We know what life looks like from the safe perspective of hindsight. In truth, we prefer the view because it includes our loved one. If we are honest, for a while, we are not particularly interested in what lies ahead. Until we are ready, it feels uncomfortable and perhaps a little frightening to think about our life without the one we love.

If you have ever experienced motion sickness, you know that it takes more than a little intestinal fortitude to ride backward. I get queasy just thinking about the disequilibrium of moving forward and riding backward at the same time. Motion sickness occurs when the eyes, inner ear, and body send conflicting messages to the brain when one is sitting still yet in motion, whether one is riding in a vehicle, boat, or airplane, experiencing an amusement park ride, or playing video or virtual reality games. Motion sickness causes us to feel weak and disoriented, temporarily out of control.

When we grieve, suddenly we are forced to take a backward-facing seat in life. The journey of grief is about the push/pull of backward and forward, past and present. Grief requires the same iron stomach needed to ride backward. The conflicted emotions of grief signal both our senses and our brain that our life is in a state of disruption, that we are, in effect, riding backward.

For a while, we experience the discomfort and emotional confusion of riding backward. Before we reach our destination, we stop at many of the stations of grief—sadness, fear, anxiety, and worry to name only a few. As we travel toward our getting off place, we reach a transfer point. There, we change seats and face forward again in life. We glimpse our life ahead with a different view to the world.

At the end of the journey, we are better for having had the backward-facing view. We know now exactly where we have been and see more clearly where we are going, "Let your eyes look directly forward and your gaze be straight before you" (Proverbs 4:25). One day, we are no longer riding backward in grief. At last, we have a forward-facing view of life again. We trust God to guide us toward the future; we move ahead into the light of new life.

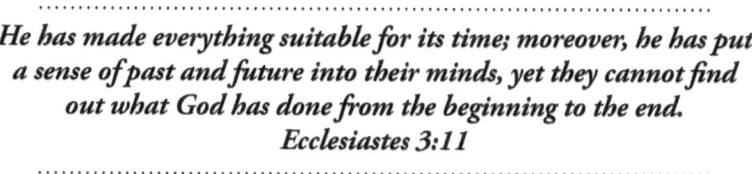

He has made everything suitable for its time; moreover, he has put a sense of past and future into their minds, yet they cannot find out what God has done from the beginning to the end.
Ecclesiastes 3:11

WHERE DO I FIT IN?

One of the subtle shifts we experience when one we love dies is reordering our place in life. Often we struggle to establish a stand-alone identity apart from that of our loved one. We agonize and wonder, "Where do I fit in?"

When the parent of an adult child dies, some grieve the loss of a beloved mother or father who has served as a role model in life. Others grieve the absence of a relationship if, over a lifetime, a parent has failed to set an example of loving actions, words, and deeds. When a parent dies in the natural course of aging, more often than not, the adult child is already well-established in life and no longer needs the affirmation or rejection of a parent to validate his or her own self-perception.

As an adult, generally we know what our life is about. We are past the point of needing to spend time and energy finding our own identity. We know who we are, for better or for worse. Usually, we know our place in life and where we fit in. When a parent dies, the spiritual standard for grief is a question of the heart that requires introspection, contemplation, and resolution, rather than a yes/no answer, "Honor your father and your mother, that your days may be long in the land which the LORD your God gives you" (Exodus 20:12 RSV).

Every child, whatever his or her age, is an active source of love and joy in life. When a child dies—in utero, as a newborn or infant, as a growing toddler or precocious child, as an inquiring teenager or young adult, or as a mature grown-up—grief feels catastrophic. Though there may be medical reasons that explain the cause of death, clinical information does little to mitigate profound grief. Grief caused by the death of a child is often rife with unanswerable questions. Grief for a child is like no other grief in life. Inevitably those who grieve the death of a child spend some part of the rest of their lives wondering what their child would look like and who he or she would have become. They think about it every day and ask "why?"

As a parent, when a child dies part of our identity is lost. There is a gaping hole in our life and an emptiness in our soul. A child is forever a part of us—body, soul, mind, and spirit. Though we survive and function, the pieces of our life never quite fit together again as neatly as before. Someone is missing. Something is broken—our heart.

When a beloved child dies, our place in the world as a parent is suddenly skewed. Other parents offer sympathy and comfort, yet suddenly we are no longer part of play groups, birthday parties, or other shared events that once included our child. We find ourself on the periphery of life, our nose pressed against the window of our former joy as a loving, devoted, engaged parent. When we are included in an activity or we are invited to a celebration, in pain-filled moments we ask ourself, "Where do I fit in?" We look around and see that our child is no longer part of all that once was. We realize that our unique place as the parent of that absent child is no more. We grieve all over again for what will never be.

When a beloved husband or wife dies, life falls apart on a grand scale. I know. Without any real warning, my husband got sick and died in a summer's span of ninety days. When he died, part of me died. I had no idea who I was or what I was supposed to do without him by my side.

Many husbands and wives have a similar experience when a beloved spouse dies. Most have spent the majority of their adult life in a relationship, the majority in a marriage. When a wife dies, more often than not, men find themselves helpless and desperately lonely. When a husband dies, many women struggle not only with loneliness but with managing the responsibilities of daily life that were once shared. When a same-sex partner, wife, or husband dies, often the emotions of grief are compounded. Friends they have enjoyed together are suddenly at a loss. They have no guidelines for how to be together with the surviving spouse. There exists a certain social imbalance, a kind of unintentional "odd person out" awkwardness that may feel insensitive and isolating. With good reason, a surviving husband, wife, or partner may ask, "Where do I fit in?"

God knows our struggle to find our identity and purpose in life without the one we love. God is continuously at work in our life to form us, mold us, and reshape us into the person we will yet become. Though we are forever changed by the death of one we love, our place in the divine order of God's creation is secure. Whatever our stage or place in life, we fit into God's perfect plan of creation.

....

For I know the plans I have for you," declares the LORD, "plans to prosper you and not to harm you, plans to give you hope and a future."
Jeremiah 29:11 NIV

....

The Distractions
of Duty

Whether you are a primary, hands-on caregiver or someone who is forced by geography or circumstance to manage the care of a loved one from afar or you oversee the care provided by professionals in an institutional setting, you do the work of love when you do the work of duty.

For some, duty is a legal obligation. For others, it is a moral obligation. For others, duty is the sacred responsibility inherent in many relationships. Whether we respond to our duty gladly or reluctantly, the demands of duty recur every day like clockwork. Duty is a harsh, unforgiving taskmaster that regiments our life and always demands more. Unless we blatantly choose to neglect it, a sense of duty can be a persistent, compelling distraction in our day-to-day life.

A few years after my husband died, I began to pray and think seriously about moving to a smaller home. It made little sense to maintain a house that was much too big for one person. After weighing the options, I found a condominium in a newer building convenient to my work, neighborhood services, and church. I closed the deal, hired a contractor, and began the months-long process of renovation needed before I could move in.

Though my mother had been in decline for several years, I was her sole caregiver. Later, I managed her care team. Her condition accelerated at about the same time that I was preparing to move. The crisis came late one afternoon when the call came that my mother had fallen. I dropped everything and went into crisis mode to ensure her care and comfort at this turning point in her life.

In the remaining months and weeks before she died, I was awash not only in duty, but also in distractions. My life seems frayed and off balance. The distractions of duty sapped my physical and emotional strength. The demands of duty drove a wedge into my spiritual being. I chased order and peace, yet there was no predictable rhythm to life. I felt as though I was idling in neutral, going nowhere—not forward, not backward. It seemed impossible to keep up with the demands of constant adjustment to circumstances beyond my control. I needed more hours than just the regulation twenty-four to keep my head above the water line.

When we grieve, often we neglect our own self-care because we are focused on the distractions of duty. We prioritize what is necessary and vital—caring for our children and family, dealing with the business of death, making wise, timely decisions.

When we are in caregiver/survival mode, we put others first and ourself last. Though for a while it is possible to do an end run around grief, it is impossible to ignore grief altogether in the hope that someday it will run its course and go away. Grief insists that we find the undistracted time and space needed to look inward. Grief urges us to confront and express our feelings. Grief encourages us to cry, mourn, and be sad. Grief is a time to attend to our mental, physical, emotional, and spiritual needs. Grief is a deeply personal experience of the heart, one that precludes both duty and distraction.

How do we access this private, personal place of grief when we are distracted by duty and life going on around us? We put down the phone, turn off the radio and television, block the loud messaging of social media, and listen to what silence has to say to us—at home, in the car, at work, or in a crowded train, bus, or subway.

Our soul is a singular space for personal reflection and introspection. It is available to us any time, any place, in any circumstance. When we lay down our duty and distraction for a while, we find the stillness needed to retreat into ourself and discover our inmost being. We need quiet to think, sort out our feelings, and experience our pain. We need quiet if we are to understand and reconcile our experience of death to the reality of life in the here and now.

We are not superhuman. We care for ourself when we ask for help. Sometimes we simply cannot do everything ourself. When others offer help and really mean it, it is the better part of self-care to delegate our duties for a while and allow others to minister to us. A momentary reprieve from duty allows us to enjoy the blessings of solitude and silence. According to Henri Nouwen, "Solitude, where we absent ourself from the myriad voices that tell us otherwise, helps us hear again that voice of love."[8]

When we seek respite from the distractions of duty, we better hear the voice of God. Through the power and presence of the Holy Spirit, God speaks comfort and peace to our soul, "Now may the Lord of peace himself give you peace at all times in all ways" (2 Thessalonians 3:16).

In quietness and confidence shall be your strength.
Isaiah 30:15 NKJV

Tiredness grounds me
Into a quiet stupor
of the spirit.

I yearn to be inspired,
to be lifted up, set free
beyond the place of deadness.

the struggle goes on,
however,
and you and I, God,
we exist together
with seemingly
little communion.

yet in the deepest part of me,
I believe in you,
perhaps more strongly than ever.

I am learning you
as a God of silence,
of darkness, deep and strong.

I do not wrestle anymore,
only wait, only wait,
for you to bring my dry bones
into dancing once again.[9]

CHANGE

E ven though I am an avowed technology geek, I have always
preferred a small personal notebook rather than an electronic
device for keeping my calendar, addresses, thoughts, reminders, and the all-important to-do list. The idea of entering information into a gizmo has never really appealed to me. I like real paper, a
good pen, and a sturdy pocket binder.

Usually, around the first of the year, I spend some time reviewing
the calendar from the previous year. It always strikes me how many
large and small changes have occurred over a year's time. When we
look back, we see where we have been. When we begin a new year,
we get a glimpse of where we might be headed. When we take the
long view, what we see is that over time, inevitably, there is change.

When we grieve, for a while the calendar seems somewhat ir-
relevant. We benchmark our life to the date on which our loved one
died. We inscribe it on our heart and remember it not only as the
date of death but perhaps as importantly, as the last day of our life as
we have known it. For with a final breath, everything changes. Nothing will ever be the same again.

When my husband was diagnosed, his illness became the sole
focus of our life. For me, time seemed to stop. The calendar meant
nothing except one day after another of slow, steady decline toward
his inevitable death. After he died, someone asked me about a world
event which occurred during that year, a time that for me stood still,
or so it seemed. Without much thought, I replied, "Oh, I missed the
spring that year." In truth, I have little recollection of anything that

happened during that space in time other than being drawn into a vortex of constant change.

When we consider the dramatic, irrevocable changes that have occurred in our life since the death of our loved one, we discern many of the ways that change continues to shape our life in the here and now. The change we attribute to death and grief slowly reveals our unique, God-given strengths. As human beings, we are endowed with a certain tenacity of spirit that moves us continuously along the adjustment curve of change in life. At the same time, our self-perception shifts. We grow and mature through the experience of grief as a constant of change.

The universal outcome of grief is a changed perspective on life. Whatever our experience of death and grief, we are forced to change. The choice is whether we grow and live or spend the rest of our life waiting to die, "Turn, O LORD, save my life; deliver me for the sake of your steadfast love" (Psalm 6:4).

The steadfast love of God is with us as we struggle and wrestle with change. The steadfast love of God is exactly that—steady, "Let your steadfast love, O LORD, be upon us, even as we hope in you" (Psalm 33:22). Our hope, our life depends on the changeless love of God.

*** For I the Lord do not change.***
*** Malachi 3:6***

COMFORT

C omfort is an experience. If comfort is an experience, how do we feel it? Most who grieve turn to those they love for comfort. Your comforter may be a parent, a spouse, a friend, or anyone who knows and meets you in your grief with insight into your soul.

My father was my great comforter. He knew how to reach into my heart with his tender comfort and care. When I was a little girl, he would unfold his large white handkerchief, dab my cheeks, wipe away my tears, and gently murmur, "Don't cry, Julie baby, don't cry." As he kissed away my hurt, he comforted me as no one else could. What I remember most about his comfort is the quiet warmth of his embrace as he held me close and said, "I love you."

When we entrust the pain of our grief to others, our emotions are fragile. We are easily hurt and disappointed when we realize that someone who loves us does not understand our loss. Though our expectations are high, no one can comfort us perfectly. Over time we learn that human comfort, even the most loving, sensitive, caring comfort, is largely of the moment. We hear the words, we feel the intent, yet deep, sustained comfort does not always seep into our soul.

How, then, do we access the comfort that quiets our heart and gives strength to our spirit? In faith, we believe that God is at work in our lives to comfort us through the power of the Holy Spirit, the Great Comforter, "And I will pray the Father, and He shall give you another Comforter, that he may be with you for ever" (John 14:16 ASV).

A few months after my husband died, I was at a gas station late one afternoon filling the car. A stranger approached and introduced herself. She said that she knew me, but I did not know her. Though my first instinct was to withdraw, her words touched me at a deep place in my grief. She said that my name had been on her heart and that she was praying for me. It was a powerful encounter. A complete stranger reached out unexpectedly and dared to enfold me with the grace of spiritual comfort. As she turned and left, I felt as though I had encountered an angel. Since then, there have been other moments when the power of the Holy Spirit, the Great Comforter, has blessed me with comfort through the outreach of others.

The word *comfort* is from the Latin *com fortis*, meaning *with strength*. To be comforted is to be made strong. Grief is about the transformation of sorrow into life-sustaining strength. The presence of the Holy Spirit in our life is God's love in action to comfort us, strengthen us, and restore us to life beyond this moment of grief.

> *Let your steadfast love become my comfort.*
> *Psalm 119:76 NRSV*

COMFORT...AGAIN

C omfort is a repetitive experience of grief. There is no one-time, one-size-fits-all comfort that can fix our grief and send us on our way in life. When we grieve, God persists in comfort. God comforts us again and again and again.

It is a certainty that there will be some trouble in our life. There is no way to escape it. We know what it feels like to have trouble, to be entangled in trouble, even to be in trouble. When we grieve the death of one we love, we are troubled in our mind and soul and spirit, "In this world you will have trouble. But take heart! I have overcome the world" (John 16:33 NIV). We are assured that God is able to overcome every trouble in our life and take heart. With God, comfort is never one and done. God comforts us again and again and again.

The psalmist paints a vivid picture of God's comfort, "Though you have made me see troubles, many and bitter, you will restore my life again; from the depths of the earth you will again bring me up. You will increase my honor and comfort me once again" (Psalm 71:20–21 NIV). We are assured that God will bring us up "from the depths of the earth." In modern vernacular, we might say that when we grieve, we are "in the pits." For a while, this is what grief feels like. The promise is that God will bring us out of the depths of our grief and restore us again to life.

Comfort is cumulative—over time it adds up to peace. We receive comfort again and again and again in each experience of God's grace. Comfort enfolds us when we hold a baby in our arms. We feel our heart respond in love to the sweet smell of innocence. Comfort enfolds us when we play with a child. We feel the energy and life-giving joy of carefree, undistracted love. Comfort enfolds us in the silent hug that says, "I understand, I love you, I care." Those who know best how to comfort us have themselves been comforted by God. They are at work in the world as agents of God's "again."

In a sermon on "Grief and Death," my husband said, "I can commend to you a God who loves you, who cares about you, and who will hold you in his arms if you will let him." Could there be a better description of God's desire to comfort us again and again and again? As he spoke, he poured his understanding of the power of God into the word *cares.* At the time, he could not have imagined that these words of grace would be meant for me. I am comforted again and again and again by the power of transcendent love.

The psalmist affirms that God will "increase our honor." Grief never leaves us where it finds us. Grief may leave us fearful and embittered, or it may enrich our life and enlarge our faith. If we are willing, God transforms us into better people through our experience of grief. God increases our honor and comforts us again and again and again.

You, Lord, have helped me and comforted me.
Psalm 86:17

COMFORTABLE?

In the deep darkness of grief, for a while we may be truly un-comfort-able. Our fervent desire is not so much for comfort as it is for the return of our life as it once was. We want our loved one to walk through the door and end our awkward, unfamiliar acquaintance with grief. At this uncomfortable place in grief, we simply cannot be comforted by anyone or anything.

One of the lessons grief has to teach us is that it is not humanly possible to imagine the death of a loved one or be comforted in advance. Jesus tried to comfort his disciples before his death. He promised the gift of the Holy Spirit and assured his friends of eternal life, but they did not understand what he meant. How could they? Jesus was still alive and well, present to them in body and in spirit. Though Jesus knew the how and when of his death, for his disciples the circumstances were confusing, the timeframe very short. Jesus went from triumph to tragedy in less than a week. When he died, they were in shock. They retreated unto themselves in disbelief, wounded and fearful as together they shared in the experience of deep, bewildered grief.

Like the disciples, we have no idea what it will feel like when one we love dies. As I sat at the bedside of my dying husband, I could not imagine what death would be like or how it would feel to experience his last breath and the finality of death. I could not read the foreboding written on the faces of those who came and went from his hospital room. I was oblivious to their intimations of mortality.

Despite all medical odds, I continued to hope that the nightmare of his illness would end, that he would open his eyes and say, "Come on, Jules, let's go home." As long as Leighton was alive, for me there was still hope. Even when death seems certain, against all logic and reason, it is the very nature of the human heart to hope.

Grief leaves some blots on our heart, indelible stains that fade over time but never entirely disappear. When memory-laden places and events remind us of our loved one, our heart skips directly to those moments in grief when we remember how it felt to be un-comfort-able. On a beautiful Sunday morning, the choir sang "One Faith, One Hope, One Lord." Leighton loved this anthem; it was sung at his retirement service and later at his memorial service. The music took my breath away; with the first notes, I dissolved into heartfelt tears. Unexpectedly, I was overcome by un-comfort-able grief. As I remembered my husband and recalled the significant occasions in our life associated with the music, I sensed him there beside me, loving and comforting me. In that twinkling of connection, my un-comfort-able spirit was transformed into a joyful reunion of our immortal souls.

Though we cannot prove it, at some time many who grieve have a personal experience that affirms the abiding spiritual presence of his or her loved one. Perhaps something unmistakable occurs, a sign or signal that you alone would understand. These intimate encounters of the soul assure us of the eternal presence and communion of our loved one.

The reality of the unseen is one of the means that God uses to comfort us in our grief. Within this reality, we find the definition of our faith, "Now faith is confidence in what we hope for and assurance about what we do not see" (Hebrews 11:1 NIV). When we grieve, we learn more about the power of the unseen. Through the grace of God, we are comforted. Through the grace of God, we are made comfort-able, sure of what we hope for, certain of what we do not see.

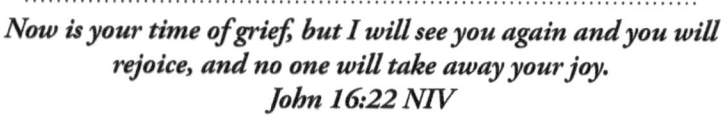

Now is your time of grief, but I will see you again and you will
rejoice, and no one will take away your joy.
John 16:22 NIV

THE WILL OF GOD?

O n our journey through grief, we strain and strive to understand the death of our loved one. Though we would like a clear, immediate answer to the "why?" of death, the wisdom of grief teaches us that the mystery of life and death is known only to God. According to Søren Kierkegaard,

> It is quite true what Philosophy says: that Life must be understood backwards. That makes one forget the other saying: that it must be lived - forwards. The more one ponders this, the more it comes to mean that life in the temporal existence never becomes quite intelligible, precisely because at no moment can I find complete quiet to take the backward-looking position.[10]

With the death of one we love comes a certain quiet, the silence that grief allows us to understand backward if indeed we are to live forward. If we listen, echoing within the silence we hear the noisy questions of grief. Did a part of me die when my loved one died? Am I dead to my own life? Is there hope that all is not lost? How do I trust in life again?

When my husband died, I wanted answers to the overarching questions of grief: Is the death of the one we love really God's will? How can tragic accidents, traumatic illness, suicide, and death from war and random violence be the will of a loving, caring God? Is death preordained by God to occur in a particular way at a specific time? Do we believe that death occurs simply at one's "appointed time"? These and other spiritual questions disquiet us when we grieve. One-way conversations of the mind and heart do little to inform our understanding of God's will. Until our questions are posed in prayer, in two-way conversation with God, we will never have answers that satisfy our soul.

Too often we toss a prayer God's way for quick affirmation of what we want. We would like for God to rubber stamp our choices with a large, red OKAY. Yet seldom do we stop to hear the answer. More often than not, we plow ahead without regard for the consequences of a self-made, rather than God-directed decision. We discount God's will with a kind of spiritual half-smile that looks like an emotional shrug, one that says, "I really do not need your help."

For a long time after Leighton's death, I struggled with "Thy will be done" in the Lord's Prayer. I asked myself what this really means when one we love dies. Leighton understood "Thy will be done" as seeking, finding, and doing the will of God, not living in passive helplessness, at the mercy of an inflictive, punitive God. In a sermon, he said, "The will of God ought to be seen as that which is positive and affirmative and active in our lives. When we pray 'Thy will be done,' we are not praying for weary resignation or forced acceptance. We are not praying to be taken out of a situation, but to be able to take it and conquer it, to defeat it and overcome it."[11]

When I paused one day on my own journey through grief to look backward, a clear answer came to me one day about my husband's death. In God's perfect timing, Leighton's days here on earth were accomplished. God's perfect plan for his life, his work, and his ministry had been fulfilled. And though questions still echo in my head and heart, our human understanding of the will of God lies in accepting the mystery of life and death. There are simply some things we will never know on this side of heaven.

When we grieve it is most certainly the will of God that we ask for and receive God's comfort. Though we may never fully understand the death of the one we love and now grieve, we trust the assurance of our faith that from death comes new life, "And the world and its desire are passing away, but those who do the will of God abide forever" (1 John 2:17).

*I know that whatever God does endures forever; nothing can be
added to it nor anything taken from it; God has done this
so that all should stand in awe before him. That which is already
has been, that which is to be already is, and God seeks out what
has gone by.*
Ecclesiastes 3:14–15

SETBACKS

When a baby learns to walk it wobbles, teeters, and occasionally falls, most often in place, squarely on its bottom. Yet with the childish courage that knows no fear, usually a toddler gets back up and tries again until it finds the equilibrium needed to stay upright and take more than a hesitant first step. In grief, we do the same—we fall down. We have setbacks, "we get knocked down" (2 Corinthians 4:9 NLT). Yet like a small child, we get up and try again.

When we grieve, there is an unaccustomed imbalance in our life, a kind of sensory vertigo that affects both mind and heart. Though we cling to the past, we are alive in the present. In this state of emotional pitch and sway, we are particularly susceptible to setbacks in our grief.

One of the assumptions of grief is that we are supposed to do something to help ourself. But when one we love dies, we have no idea what it is we are supposed to do. Grief does not come with a how-to manual or instruction booklet. Many onlookers to our grief feel free to offer unsolicited advice about what we *should* do. Very few suggestions that begin with *should* are helpful when we grieve.

- "You should have more faith."
- "You should pull yourself together."
- "You should give away his or her clothes."
- "You should get on with your life."

When my husband died, I had no idea how to piece my life back together again. In an effort to do something to help myself, I tried on new things, new places, and new people. For a long while, I experienced more setbacks than success. I had no idea what I needed to do to get it right. For a while, my efforts felt like a colossal flop.

Every setback had an effect on my suffering spirit. At first, I was devastated by each large and small failure. Over time, I learned to dust myself off, laugh a little, and learn something from each encounter with change and life as it was becoming. Slowly but surely, I managed to assemble the one thousand pieces of my personal jigsaw puzzle until the picture entitled "the rest of my life" began to take shape.

When we grieve, setbacks are a certainty. For a while, all we can do is pull up our socks and try—again and again. When setbacks occur, often they feel like the complete undoing of our hard-won progress in grief. It seems as though we take one step forward in grief followed by two steps backward. Setbacks reminds us that our gains in grief are incremental. Imperceptibly, over time, grief becomes two steps forward and one step backward.

Setbacks are part of the rhythm of grief. It is not unusual to experience a setback at the holiday season or on a remembrance day. When we revisit our grief on the occasions of life, often setbacks feel as though we have fallen back into the valley with little hope of climbing out again. It is easy to think about giving up on life when we experience setbacks. But when we try and do the work of grief, we regain our footing and move forward again, grateful for the life that is ours to live. More often than not, we find the antidote to setbacks in the restorative power of sleep, prayer, and a new day, "He gives strength to the weary and increases the power of the weak" (Isaiah 40:29 NIV).

You have struggled with God and with humans
and have overcome.
Genesis 32:28 NIV

STUCK

While driving down the freeway one day in early December, my mind was going in what seemed like a thousand different directions—holiday preparations, Christmas travel, year-end business, and on and on. Though I seldom listen to the radio in the car, the news was on because I wanted to hear the weather report.

Before the hourly update, there was an interview with a woman who had been in the thick of the so-called Black Friday shopping melee. From what she said, evidently she was torn between the secular and the spiritual. The interviewer asked how she would celebrate the holidays, to which she replied, "I'm stuck in the middle of my wants." Her answer got my attention.

To be stuck in the middle of our wants is a thought worth pondering, especially when we grieve. Though from time to time we experience what we think of as setbacks in our grief, in truth we may be stuck. More often than not, the feeling of being stuck is usually only a short-lived interlude caused by low mental, physical, or emotional energy. We idle for a while, address whatever issue has brought us to a halt on our journey, refill our tank, find our momentum, and move forward again in grief.

If we are stuck in the middle of our wants, we set ourself up for frustration and disappointment. We want what we want, and we want it now. Getting unstuck in grief starts with assessing our wants. Getting unstuck is about putting away wants that can never be fulfilled. Getting unstuck is about identifying wants that are possible and attainable. Consider whether these wants are realistic or whether are you stuck in the middle of your wants.

- You want life to be as it once was.
- You want to climb out of the emotional hole of grief.
- You want to feel better and reconnect with life.
- You want to look ahead.
- You want to know what the future holds.
- You want to know when your grief will be over.
- You want to find a positive dynamic for the rest of your life.
- You want to experience love and joy again in your life.

When we are stuck in grief, we see life only through a small knothole. Our limited perspective suggests that the emotional ambivalence we feel now is how our life will always be. How do we get unstuck? Getting unstuck is about persevering in grief. Getting unstuck is about praying with expectation. Getting unstuck is about accessing God's plan for the rest of our life. Getting unstuck is about living in and living into the promise of God's presence with renewed hope, recovered love, and belief in the future.

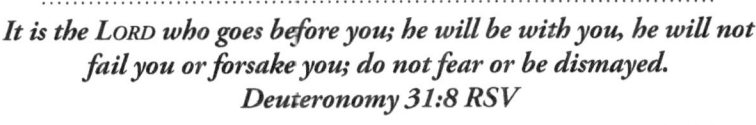

It is the LORD who goes before you; he will be with you, he will not fail you or forsake you; do not fear or be dismayed.
Deuteronomy 31:8 RSV

GRACE LIGHT

And after you have suffered for a little while, the God of all grace, who has called you to his eternal glory in Christ, will himself restore, support, strengthen, and establish you.

1 Peter 5:10

GRACE

s a child, I was taken to church at least three times a week to
learn about God. The beliefs of the denomination empha-
sized guilt, shame, and a laundry list of suggestive sins that
were denounced each week in the sermon. From a very early age, my
understanding of God was based on learned fear.

It was not until early adulthood that I first heard the word grace.
In a sermon, a United Methodist minister, Dr. Leighton Farrell,
explained the meaning of grace—God's love unearned, unmerited,
and undeserved. He did so with deep theological understanding. He
did so with a conviction born of personal experience. Years later, he
would become my husband.

Grace was an unfamiliar, almost inconceivable concept to me.
After years of conditioning in fear, it was slow work to grow into the
idea of grace as the gift of God's love, a gift from the One who is love,
"There is no fear in love, but perfect love casts out fear; for fear has to
do with punishment, and whoever fears has not reached perfection
in love" (1 John 4:18–19).

An understanding of grace is something that grows, expands,
and becomes richer over the course of a lifetime. Grace is a living
experience that unites our heart with the heart of God. If we are attuned to moments when God speaks to us clearly and unmistakably,
we recognize grace. Grace is the highest expression of God's love for
humankind. Grace intimates the power and presence of God at work
in our life.

Our human capacity to understand the limitless nature of God's
love is elevated by every experience of grace in our life, "For my

thoughts are not your thoughts, nor are your ways my ways, says the LORD. For as the heavens are higher than the earth, so are my ways higher than your ways and my thoughts than your thoughts" (Isaiah 55:8–9). When we see God's love in action and feel God's unearned, unmerited, and undeserved love, we experience the power of grace. This is about as close to God as we can ever hope to be on this side of heaven.

In the overblown rhetoric of the internet, "amazing" has become one of the most prosaic words in the English language. The hymn we know as "Amazing Grace" with words by John Newton (1725–1807) was inspired by a life-altering personal experience of grace in his life.

Newton grew up without any particular religious conviction. He was conscripted into service in the Royal Navy at an early age and later became involved in the Atlantic slave trade. In 1748, a violent storm battered his vessel so severely that he called out to God for mercy. Though this experience marked his spiritual conversion, he continued in the slave trade until 1755. When his seafaring career came to an end, he began a rigorous study of Christian theology and subsequently became an Anglican clergyman, a poet, and an impassioned abolitionist.

With its message of forgiveness and redemption through the mercy and grace of God, "Amazing Grace" is one of the most beloved songs in the English-speaking world. It was my father's favorite hymn; if I close my eyes, I can hear him sing it, even now.

> Amazing grace! (how sweet the sound)
> That sav'd a wretch like me!
> I once was lost, but now am found,
> Was blind, but now I see.

> 'Twas grace that taught my heart to fear,
> And grace my fears reliev'd;
> How precious did that grace appear
> The hour I first believ'd!

Thro' many dangers, toils, and snares,
I have already come;
'Tis grace hath brought me safe thus far,
And grace will lead me home.

The Lord has promis'd good to me,
His word my hope secures;
He will my shield and portion be
As long as life endures.

Yes, when this flesh and heart shall fail,
And mortal life shall cease;
I shall possess, within the veil,
A life of joy and peace.

The earth shall soon dissolve like snow,
The sun forbear to shine;
But God, who call'd me here below,
Will be forever mine.[12]

Until that day when our relationship with God becomes that of a different realm, there will be trials, struggles, tests, and temptations in this world. Through the power of grace, we overcome the adversities of life. Through grace, amazing grace, we experience sacred relationship with the God of all grace. There is no circumstance of separation, lost relationship, death, or life that cannot be overcome by the extravagant grace of God.

From his fullness we have all received, grace upon grace.
John 1:16

HEALING OUR WOUNDS

There is no disappointment or betrayal in life that has the same power to crush our spirit as death.

The summer that I cleaned out my mother's house, before I began, I whispered a prayer for God's strength and guidance. To prepare for the task, I got what seemed like a truckload of boxes, several rolls of packing paper, bubble wrap, and a dozen or more rolls of heavy-duty tape. Each day, I put on my work clothes, gloves, and comfortable shoes. By the time the job was done, there was a large hole in the sole of my left shoe.

Soon I found a rhythm—decide, dispose, decide, discard. I had a mantra I repeated to myself several times a day, "the job is finite, the job is finite." Despite my ability to organize and a personal commitment to dispose of each thing with care and respect, the job was laden with emotion. As I labored and toiled, I reflected on our flawed, damaged relationship. At the end of ten dawn-to-dusk days, the work was over but my grief was not.

After the heavy lifting was done, I inspected the wounds on my body. There was hardly a square inch on my arms and legs that did not have a bruise, scrape, bump, or scratch. I blamed the injuries on the bulky things I had touched, toted, boxed, and moved. I knew that it would take a week or more for the bruises to fade and the scratches to heal. I hoped there would be no scars to remind me of that thankless task. Notwithstanding my visible wounds, a large emotional blotch lingered in my heart and soul.

When one we love dies, we are wounded. We hurt. We are in pain. We want our broken heart no longer to feel so broken. We wonder whether it is even possible for a broken heart to be healed. Though at times we doubt whether we want to be healed, somewhere deep within our soul, we long for healing, the healing that comes only from God, "For he wounds, but he binds up; he strikes, but his hands heal" (Job 5:18).

If we are physically injured, we bind up our wounds because we want to relieve the pain. We believe that in time, our wounds will heal. When we grieve, we experience not only wounds to our heart caused by the death of one we love but also wounds to our spirit caused by imperfect relationships that fester in our soul.

Although there is no intimation of quid pro quo in God's promise of healing, logic implies that healing begins with spiritual self-help. When we grieve, we must do our part to prepare for God's healing. We prepare a clean heart when we purge our heart of bitterness, resentment, and disappointment, a sterile field ready for God to bind up our wounds. If we fail to do our part to facilitate healing—forgiving, forgetting, releasing the past—the wounds of grief can leave us emotionally scarred and spiritually disfigured for life.

Whether our wounds are physical, emotional, mental, or spiritual, God promises that our broken heart will be healed. We access God's healing power through prayer. In communion with God, we share the pain of our brokenness. In fulfillment of God's promise, our broken heart is healed, "He heals the brokenhearted and binds up their wounds" (Psalm 147:3). We are healed from the wounds of grief through the grace of God.

....

For I will restore health to you, and your wounds
I will heal, says the LORD.
Jeremiah 30:17

....

HEALING FROM GRIEF

I s there healing from grief? Do we ever really recover from grief? The answer is both yes and no, for in some way, we are forever marked by the experience of death and grief. Just as a wound leaves an imperfection on our physical body, grief leaves a scar on our heart. Though gradually it fades and becomes less noticeable, a tender reminder of the death of one we love remains with us always.

Death wounds our heart, our soul, and our spirit. The greater our love for the one we have loved and lost, the larger and deeper our wound. For some, the wound is caused by a slow leave-taking over months or years of chronic illness. For others, there is a large, open wound when the death of a loved one is sudden or tragic. The pain is so acute that we cannot imagine ever being healed from grief.

When we grieve, we triage and treat our brokenness with care and sensitivity because only we know how it feels to experience the death of one we love. Though a counselor, therapist, or trained professional can offer mental and emotional first aid through listening and support, God alone is the great physician, God alone can heal us from our grief.

Healing begins with a decision: Do I want to live the rest of my life with a heart that is permanently broken? Healing begins only when we can affirm to ourself that we want to be made well. In John 5:2–9, we read the story of a man who wanted to be healed but was helpless. This man had been an invalid for thirty-eight years. Physically, he was unable to get into the pool of Bethesda, which was thought to have healing powers. He waited beside the pool every day in the hope that someone would help him get into the water so that he might be healed of his lifelong infirmity. The question we must ask ourself is the same one put to the man, "Do you want to be made well?"

Healing is for those who want to be made well. Healing is for those who desire wholeness and restoration to life. Healing is for those who have hope for the future. Healing is for those willing to do the work of introspection and forgiveness needed to reclaim a life of unconstrained joy.

Can you imagine how it would feel to be healed from grief? Like any rehabilitation from injury or illness, healing requires commitment, fortitude, and courage. As we seek to rehabilitate ourself from the experience of grief, we stretch and grow. We become stronger than our grief when we reclaim a life that is healthy and whole.

For a while, we must convalesce and recuperate from grief. We reach a turning point in our healing when we are less focused on the pain of grief and more intent on acceptance of the death of one we love. For some, learning to live alongside the death of a loved one may open the door that leads toward recovery and healing from grief.

As we near the end of grief, the full incorporation of the death of one we love into our living, breathing, daily existence allows us to experience God's healing from grief. With self-understanding we see clearly that his or her death will be part of our life forever—who we are now and who we will yet become. We will always love; we will never forget.

Healing from grief does not happen overnight. As with the human body, it takes time, tender care, and attention before we are well and whole again after the death of one we love. In the fullness of time, God heals us from grief; God heals our broken heart, "for I am the LORD who heals you" (Exodus 15:26).

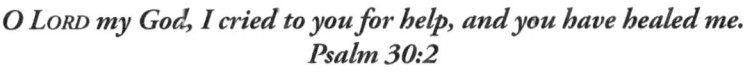

O LORD my God, I cried to you for help, and you have healed me.
Psalm 30:2

THE HAND

Often the things we see when we are driving get our attention. The behavior, temperament, and manners of others is a kind of mobile life lesson. One day at a stop light, I saw a driver with one hand draped casually over the steering wheel. In his other hand about 20 inches from his face, he was gripping a phone. He was staring at it intently, talking and gesturing as though the other person was sitting in the car next to him. Perhaps he was using Facetime. Clearly he was in the middle of an intense conversation. The intimacy of his exchange was fascinating. He was the definition of a distracted driver.

Likely most everyone has been in an elevator or social situation where the use of a cell phone precludes any other human engagement. If we are the offender, often we are oblivious to anything or anyone beyond the thing in our hand. A bowed head signals total immersion in the images and sounds of a device. Do not disturb. The glow of the screen casts an eerie shadow, the person staring at the phone looks surreal, dehumanized, and robotic.

The hands are perhaps the most tactile part of the human body. The nerve endings in our hands allow us to feel and touch and sense far beyond the visual. Hands are designed to perform fine motor skills that enable us to write and sew and create and caress and throw a baseball. Our hands reach out to hold the hands of another in love and comfort. Through touch, we connect to others in wordless trust.

When we grieve, we reach out to God with the hands of our heart and soul, "my eye grows dim through sorrow. Every day I call on you, O LORD; I spread out my hands to you" (Psalm 88:9). My husband and I always held hands whenever we were together. God now holds both his hand and mine, forever bound by the warmth of a great earthly love, "The Lord is your keeper; the Lord is your shade at your right hand" (Psalm 121:5). God never lets go of our hands; God's hand upholds us when we grieve, "My soul clings to you; your right hand upholds me" (Psalm 63:8).

I am left-handed. Since the death of my husband, I have found special comfort in the image of God's strong right hand holding my left hand, my hand of greatest strength and greatest weakness, "do not fear, for I am with you; do not be afraid, for I am your God; I will strengthen you; I will help you; I will uphold you with my victorious right hand" (Isaiah 41:10).

God knows the needs of our hands and heart when we grieve. We are assured that we are in God's hands, "But you do see! Indeed, you note trouble and grief, that you may take it into your hands; the helpless commit themselves to you" (Psalm 10:14).

We cannot see God's hand holding ours, yet we feel it when our heart knows without a shadow of doubt that God is with us, beside us, lighting the way through our experience of grief. We have only to put our hand into the hand of God. Hand in hand, God shows us the path of life.

You show me the path of life. In your presence there is fullness of joy; in your right hand are pleasures forevermore.
Psalm 16:11

THE HEART

A few months after a new grief support group for surviving spouses began at the church, an elegant gentleman came for the first time. His heart was broken because of the recent death of his beloved wife. He shared with the group that in their marriage, each had a clearly defined role. He was a clothing executive and earned their living. His wife took care of him and their children. In the context of their roles, he knew how life went, until his wife was diagnosed with a terminal illness. When she died, her husband found himself suddenly quite alone. He was unable to function and cope without the care and support of his wife. Though he was perceptive and intelligent, he was clueless about how to make a cup of coffee or a meal for himself or what it takes to have clean socks.

Dick joined the group because of his helplessness and crushing sense of loneliness. He hoped to find friends who would understand his loss. He needed to tell his story. He needed to talk out loud about his challenges and know that others were listening. He needed to be heard. He attended faithfully and contributed some interesting insights about his personal experience of grief. The group was a community of care for him because everyone was suffering from what seemed at the time like incurable heartbreak.

No one was aware that he had a problem with his physical heart. One day, someone called to say that he was in the hospital. When I went to visit him, he mentioned that a staff member from the church had called to check on him. She asked whether the stress of his grief might be contributing to his condition. For him, this was a new thought. He had never considered the possibility that in some way his emotional heartache might have contributed to his heart attack. Gratefully, he recovered his physical health. His hospital stay made him realize that he needed to make some life changes. To recover from the stress on his heart caused by his experience of grief and restore his hope for the future, he moved to a retirement community. There, he had regular housekeeping and meal service. There, he made new friends and found the social support he needed.

It is a medical fact that the stress of grief can affect our heart. Often we are aware that our heart is beating faster than normal when we experience emotional distress. We feel our blood pressure rise. We feel tense, irritable, and out of sorts.

After my husband died, I had several grief-induced panic attacks that felt like I was having a heart attack. I called them stress attacks. My heart pounded, I was short of breath, I felt nauseated, sick all over, and shed copious tears. These episodes recurred for a while with alarming regularity. Usually they were triggered by sights, sounds, smells, people, and places that I associated with my husband's illness and death.

For several months, I could do little to control the familiar symptoms when panic overwhelmed my heart. In time, I learned to interrupt spontaneous bouts of tears with a drink of cold water before I had a complete meltdown. As I began to understand more about stress and panic attacks and how they affect the physical heart, over time they subsided.

We learn from grief that in the heart we find our inmost spiritual connection to God. God cares about our broken heart, "The LORD is near to the brokenhearted and saves the crushed in spirit" (Psalm 34:18). God guards our heart, "And the peace of God, which surpasses all understanding, will guard your hearts and your minds in Christ Jesus" (Philippians 4:7). God strengthens our heart, "My flesh and my heart may fail, but God is the strength of my heart and my portion forever" (Psalm 73:26).

When we grieve, it is not unusual for our body to respond in physical ways to a heart that is broken by the death of one we love,

"My heart is in anguish within me; the terrors of death have fallen upon me" (Psalm 55:4). The life-giving oxygen of God's comfort allows us to breathe in God's love and care. Through the power of hope, God revives the grief-weary spirit and restores our broken heart to the grace of God's perfect wholeness.

Guard your heart above all else, for it determines the course of your life.
Proverbs 4:23 NLT

THE MIND

Grief is perhaps the least cerebral experience we will ever have in life. Try though we might, grief cannot be managed or conquered by the discipline of our mind or the force of our will. When we grieve, we experience first-hand the interdependence of our mind and heart. The mind reads the heart to tell us what we feel and what we need. When we grieve, the mind cannot lead. It must follow the heart.

Not long after my husband died, almost every Saturday afternoon, I found myself in some bookstore or another sitting on a library stool in front of the shelf dedicated to books on grief. I thought that if I could just read something about grief and understand what I was feeling, I would somehow get it and be better. The intellectual approach to my pain and deep sorrow did not work—at all. I would purchase five books, toss aside three, and read two.

I read about grief as a clinical study, grief for survival, and grief as personal stories. I hungered for substance and comfort, yet nothing I read filled my emptiness. Though I gleaned a word here and a thought there, I realized that I was looking for more—something deep, lasting, and spiritual. Intuitively, I knew that the disconnect between my mind and heart must be restored if I were to survive the experience of grief.

When our heart is broken by the death of one we love, reconnecting the emotional, physical, mental, and spiritual parts of ourself feels like a daunting task. Though everyone does the work of grief differently, at some time we must look within and discern the needs of our inmost self. We are forced by grief to examine what we think and how we feel about the death of our loved one. Even when our life seems to be at a standstill, our mind is working and thinking, seeking answers and insight to inform our grief.

Reassembling my heartbroken self has been a spiritual journey, one that I chronicled in a journal. Over several years, I have recorded my thoughts and feelings. Ideas and reflections that surprise me have poured out and onto the page. When we grieve, our mind listens to our heart with rapt attention. In communion with God, our mind directs our spiritual and emotional understanding of death and grief.

When one we love dies, our mind is filled with the static noise of grief. Only when we silence the distractions can we reconnect our head and heart. We renew our mind not from without but from within, "Do not be conformed to this age, but be transformed by the renewing of the mind, so that you may discern what is the will of God—what is good and acceptable and perfect" (Romans 12:2).

As we do the work of grief, we seek to renew our mind. We move forward in grief when our mind perceives that God is at work reconnecting the broken parts of our soul and spirit. We are transformed by the renewing of our mind when we discern the good, acceptable, and perfect will of God for our life, now and for our life beyond this time of grief.

You shall love the Lord your God with all your heart
and with all your soul and with all your mind.
Matthew 22:37

RECORD KEEPING

During tornado season in Texas, it is not unusual for entire communities to suffer major destruction. In a matter of seconds, homes are leveled, personal belongings are destroyed, and people die. We are shocked by the suddenness of death. We mourn those who die and all that is lost. We grieve both collectively and individually.

When those who survive begin to reassemble their lives from whatever remains, usually it is not the real estate they grieve. Houses can be rebuilt. It is the record of their life that they grieve—the irreplaceable photos, memorabilia, letters, and keepsakes that tell the story of their family history that can never be replaced or recovered.

By nature, we are hard-wired to be record keepers. We keep a calendar, write notes, make lists, and send memos. We text, message, and email, often with a photo or video attached. For many, it is a source of pleasure to create a daily record of the events of life. Some find pleasure in the dying art of personal correspondence—writing a letter on a beautiful piece of paper with a real fountain pen. Sometimes family and friends who receive our letters save them. I kept many of the notes people wrote to me when my husband died. They are an enduring record of how people felt about him, the difference he made in life, and his lasting legacy to others.

The psalmists were nothing-held-back record keepers. They wrote what they felt. They cried out, they lamented, they wept, they grieved, they rejoiced, they praised God, "Record my misery; list my tears on your scroll—are they not in your record?" (Psalm 56:8 NIV).

Three weeks after Leighton died, I was overwhelmed by a sense of emotional desperation. I felt as though I might explode. I urgently needed an outlet to defuse the extreme pain and intensity of my grief. At the time, I was not ready to seek the help of a counselor or therapist. Intuitively, I knew that I must find a way to express my pent-up sorrow. I knew as well that if I did not release the agitation, anxiety, and despair I was internalizing every minute of every day, likely there would be some dire physical or mental consequence. At the time, the possibility of a heart attack or stroke seemed very real to me.

I am certain it was the Holy Spirit that directed me to the bookstore to buy a journal that day. Until then, I had never even kept a diary. Though personal writing was new for me, the journal became my mental lifeline. It saved my sanity through months of shock and dark grief.

As I turned to page one and began to write, the floodgates of my soul opened. I poured the anguish of my heart, my mind, and my wounded spirit onto page after page after page of my journal, every day for many months. When at last I paused to read what I had written, I found that I had made a record of what happened when my husband died and how I felt about it. In effect, I had told the story of his illness and death and my experience of grief to myself. I still journal, though differently and not as often. In my current journal, I write random thoughts, inspirational ideas, and surprising stray scraps of lingering grief.

Although journaling is not for everyone, when we keep a personal record of our life, usually we feel relief when we release our thoughts, especially when it comes to our narrative of grief. What we find is that our inner voice has something to say to us about life and death, love and death, as well as death and grief. When we write down what we feel, we listen to the voice of our inmost heart. No one will read what you write or how you write your story. No one will grade your personal record of grief. There is no test; grammar and punctuation do not count. A journal is private and personal.

Often journaling serves as a kind of self-help therapy that gives us insight and instructs our life.

Think. Reflect. Pray. Make some notes or write in a journal. Listen to thoughts that bubble up from the depth of your heart and soul. Whatever you sense, remember, and experience, give your emotions a place and space for expression. Tell yourself how you feel about the death of the one you love and now grieve. We honor our grief when we keep a personal record of our life. In the words of our heart, we discover more about God—God's love, God's care, God's comfort, God's perspective for life beyond this moment of grief.

In God, whose word I praise, in the LORD, whose word I praise—in God I trust and am not afraid. What can man do to me?
Psalm 56:10–11 NIV

THE SWEETNESS OF LIFE

In late February one year, the father of a dear friend died, though not unexpectedly. The memorial service was in a small town in northeast Texas at a historic old church a few blocks from the town square. Before going inside, I spotted a cornerstone tucked into an exterior architectural support and paused for a moment to read the inscription and names. I thought of the vision and sacrifice that built the church, the energy and industry that sustained it through the agricultural heyday of the community, and the challenge faced by so many churches today—to discern its mission and carry on in the world.

The day was warm and bright, and the sun streamed through the beautiful stained-glass windows, each with a story to tell. Before the service, the family stood at the front of the sanctuary and greeted those who had come from far and wide to honor the life and memory of a simple, godly man.

My friend shared with me that his father lived a good life and died a good death. I asked him what he was feeling in his heart. With tears in his eyes, he said, "I am overwhelmed by the sweetness of life." His words were the takeaway of the day for me. The sweetness of life. Life words, death words, grief words, words that remind us to live in spiritual abundance every day, especially when we grieve.

The leisurely drive home was peaceful, a quiet time to reflect on the sweetness of life. As I passed by acre after acre of freshly disked farmland, its soil moist and shiny, prepared for the next season of sowing and reaping, I thought of how we tend the soil of our life, "Sow for yourself righteousness; reap steadfast love; break up your fallow ground, for it is time to seek the LORD, that he may come and rain righteousness upon you" (Hosea 10:12). If we sow in love, we reap the sweetness of life.

The cycle of nature suggests a paradigm for what we sow and what we reap when we grieve the death of one we love, "May those who sow in tears reap with shouts of joy" (Psalm 126:5). Whatever we sow, we will reap. If we sow in tears, we will reap in joy as we live into the future beyond this time of grief.

As we experience the seasons of grief, for a while life seems more bitter than sweet. A broken heart is bitterly painful. A broken heart is easily embittered. Bittersweet memories season our expectations for the future. Despite our grief or perhaps because of our grief, we experience not bitterness, but the sweetness of life in the light of God that surrounds us with grace, "Light is sweet, and it is pleasant for the eyes to see the sun" (Ecclesiastes 11:7).

As we do the work of plowing and planting, the seeds of our grief grow and mature into renewed self-confidence and hope. When the harvest is ripe, we reap the fruits of our labor—the sweetness of life in all its goodness.

O taste and see that the LORD is good!
Happy is the man who takes refuge in him.
Psalm 34:8 RSV

STILL WATERS

Not too far from downtown Dallas, there is an urban oasis on the banks of a popular in-town lake. The Dallas Arboretum is situated on 66 acres that include two former estates. The original houses are open to the public. The lush gardens and impressive water features are meticulously maintained and continuously improved. The arboretum is a place of uncommon natural beauty enhanced by the imagination and creativity of man-made cultivation and development.

Until a few weeks before he died, my husband and I went there regularly to enjoy the peace and tranquility of this city getaway. While he was in the hospital, we received the annual notice to renew our membership. My first impulse was to cancel it. I could not imagine that we would ever go there again. To my surprise, he said, "Oh, no, renew the Arboretum." His implied confidence in the future assured me and gave me hope.

For many months after he died, I went to the arboretum to journal and grieve. For me, it was a sanctuary, a place of peace and solace where I felt somehow connected to Leighton's spirit. I found a bench, one I came to think of as my grieving bench, that to this day still reminds me of my tears and deep grief. For a while, the arboretum served as both refuge and retreat, a place where I could go to escape the chaos of the world. It was for me a sacred space beside still waters where I could commune with God and be at one with nature.

When we grieve, God leads us to a place beside still waters, wherever that may be, "He leads me beside still waters" (Psalm 23:2 RSV). God leads; we follow. Or not. God does not insist that we follow. God does not tug or push or pull us into the wake of God's love and care. If we resist, God waits patiently. When we are ready, we put our hand into the hand of God who gently leads us to a place of perfect peace beside still waters. Often we are surprised by where God leads us.

Your place beside still waters may be anywhere that gives you a momentary respite from grief. It is anywhere that you experience peace. Where is that place is for you? Though it seems counterintuitive, I experience peace when I am in the middle of the energy, noise, and crowds of New York City. There I find space beyond the limitations of myself to listen, think, and reflect.

When we are there, wherever our place is beside still waters—a lake, a pool, the seaside, the ocean, a fountain, or a bustling city—we pause. We take a breath. We listen for the voice of God. From our place beside still waters, there is a view. We see where we have been, where we are now, and the future that lies ahead.

As our shepherd, God leads us to a place of quiet beside still waters. There our souls are restored, "God, my shepherd! I don't need a thing. You have bedded me down in lush meadows, you find me quiet pools to drink from. True to your word, you let me catch my breath and send me in the right direction" (Psalm 23:1–3 MSG).

....

Then they were glad because they had quiet,
and he brought them to their desired haven.
Psalm 107:30

....

Ripples

I took a quick trip last week that was more about activity than rest. It was not exactly a vacation but more of a getaway. Before leaving the hotel, I paused for a final look out the window to take a mental photo of the natural beauty visible above and below the treetops. The pictures of the mind we make and take with us are the enduring souvenirs of our life.

There is a small man-made lake tucked into a stand of lush greenery that adds beauty and contrast to the park. Most days it is very still. That day, there was a gentle breeze rippling across the water. As the wind pushed the surface of the lake one way and then another, the ripples looked chaotic and confused. There was no predictable, rhythmic flow or direction.

We experience the same disorganized ripple effect when someone or something disturbs the tranquil surface of our daily life. The smallest ripples affect us in unexpected ways. When one we love dies, grief creates much more than a ripple effect. Every aggravation and annoyance feels like a tidal wave rather than a ripple.

The death of one we love is not a pebble tossed into the shallow end of our life. It is not a skipping stone that dances across the expanse of our life. The death of one we love is a heavy rock, a dead weight that sinks into the deep end of our life and stays there. The effect of death is that it causes a sea change in our life, a permanent shift away from our life as it once was to the reality of life in the here and now. The ebb and flow of our life is interrupted by the death of one we love. The ripples and waves of grief affect all that was once familiar and certain. For a while, we live without direction in a state of emotional chaos. The ripple effect of grief expands and spreads outward. It touches everyone and everything we hold dear.

When the effect of grief ripples then storms through our life, how do we tame the disturbance and find a center of calm? We pray and seek God, our refuge and safe haven, "God is our refuge and strength, a very present help in trouble. Therefore we will not fear, though the earth should change, though the mountains shake in the heart of the sea, though its waters roar and foam, though the mountains tremble with its tumult" (Psalm 46:1–3).

The ripples of grief subside when we still our heart, "Be still, and know that I am God!" (Psalm 46:10). God calms and quiets our soul when we grieve, "But I have calmed and quieted my soul" (Psalm 131:2).

*The L*ORD *your God is with you, he is mighty to save.*
He will take great delight in you, he will quiet you
with his love, he will rejoice over you with singing.
Zephaniah 3:17

WORDLESS GRACE

For fifteen years, I shared an office with my father. Our work relationship was one of mutual respect and understanding. He had his business, and I had mine. Day in and day out, we worked alongside each other in amiable silence. Ours was a relationship of wordless grace that required no chatter. There were days when we exchanged few words. He summed up our lifetime together in his dying words to me, "I love you."

My husband and I lived in the wordless grace of shared strength and mutual devotion. We never missed an opportunity to hold hands, sit close, or say "I love you." Many words were unsaid yet spoken through the intimacy of silence.

Once upon a time there was a beloved child, the child I never had, whose special place to cuddle was the hollow of my neck. Even as an infant, he knew that there he was safe. In the quiet, mystical love of innocence untainted by the world, we shared the trust of wordless grace.

When one we love dies, often we cannot express in words the depth of our pain and sorrow. We cannot describe how it feels to have a broken heart. Words cannot satisfy our emotional and spiritual needs. If the death of one we love is sudden, traumatic, unexpected, or especially cruel, often we are speechless. When we are in shock, there simply are no words.

When we grieve, it is not unusual to feel distant or estranged from God for a while. We do not know what to pray for or how to pray. If we have no words, often we find that our every thought is part of an ongoing stream of consciousness prayer. If we find ourself without words or unable to pray, wordless grace brings us into deep spiritual communion with God.

- When we have no words, God hears the silent prayer of our heart, "Listen to my cry, for I am in desperate need" (Psalm 142:6 NIV).

- When we have no words, God speaks to us through silence, "Be silent! Be Still!" (Mark 4:39).

- When we have no words, God hears the sighs of our heart, "O Lord, all my longing is known to you; my sighing is not hidden from you" (Psalm 38:9).

Wordless grace is one of the most profound, spiritual experiences of grief. The wordless prayer of a grieving heart is answered by God's grace and through God's grace.

Then when you call upon me and come
and pray to me, I will hear you.
Jeremiah 29:12

SEARCHING

Recently I read a favorite Scripture in a version of the Bible that is slightly different from the one I usually read. I was struck by the use of the word *search* rather than *seek*, "Ask, and it will be given to you; search, and you will find; knock, and the door will be opened for you. For everyone who asks receives, and everyone who searches finds, and for everyone who knocks, the door will be opened" (Matthew 7:7–8).

For most words in the English language, there are nuances of meaning. Searching implies the hope that something which is lost can be recovered. Seeking suggests a quest for something that is deep and lasting.

We spend much of our life searching. We use a flashlight to search every nook and cranny of our home, our car, or office for something that is lost or misplaced. As we search, our expectation is that we will find whatever it is that we have lost. We look high and low, far and wide until we are reunited with the thing that was misplaced or missing.

We use a searchlight to look for someone who is lost or missing. We listen to media reports on the progress of search and rescue missions. We search online for goods, information, and services. We search both for those that benefit our life and for those that add questionable value to our life. We spend time and energy searching for the transient things of life that come and go. Perhaps the age-old childhood game ought to be called Hide and Search rather than Hide and Seek. When the one designated to search discovers the hiding place, victory is declared, and the game is over.

When we grieve, we feel lost. We feel lost to ourself, lost to our family, and lost to the world without the one we love. We search the physical landscape of our life for remnants of his or her presence. We smell their clothes; we leaf through their books. We search for some assurance that he or she is not forever lost to our life. When my husband died, slowly my mind grasped the reality of his death. Yet my heart continued to search for some sign that his spirit was still alive and present to me in the world. I needed assurance that all was not lost, "When you search for me, you will find me; if you seek me with all your heart" (Jeremiah 29:13).

For all our searching, we find the people we love and grieve in surprising, unexpected places. We find them in the faces and lives of the next generation of our family. We find them in the example of character and integrity they have modeled for others. We find them in their lasting legacy of service to others and the world. Searching and finding, finding and searching—the cooperative work of heart and mind, soul and spirit that opens our inmost being to the presence and grace of God, "You search out my path and my lying down and are acquainted with all my ways" (Psalm 139:3).

Search me, O God, and know my heart; test me
and know my thoughts.
Psalm 139:23

SEEKING

Seeking is a lifelong endeavor that goes well beyond searching. When we seek rather than search, we look for that which is deep and intentional, that which adds meaning and purpose to our life, though our quest is often unclear. When we seek, our quest is often unclear. In truth, seeking is sometimes a hard trudge through the muck and mire of life. Seeking is about taking the first step and then the next in pursuit of whatever it is that we seek. Seeking requires persistence, spiritual fortitude, and faith in the direction and guidance of God, "And those who know your name put their trust in you, for you, O Lord, have not forsaken those who seek you" (Psalm 9:10).

Seeking is one of the challenges of grief, "For everything there is a season and a time for every matter under heaven...a time to seek and a time to lose" (Ecclesiastes 3:1, 6). When one we love dies, we must seek out a new existence for ourself, a different way to live and be in the world without the one we love. Grief is a time to seek answers to our questions about death in spiritual communion with God. We seek in the assurance that death is not the end, that there is life beyond death.

Most who grieve seek answers to some of the more complex questions of life and death. In *Cries from the Cross*, my husband wrote,

> What most of us need in our adversity is not to find an explanation—but to find a victory; it is not to elaborate a theory—but to lay hold upon a power. Even if the best and most completely satisfying answer to our question "why?" was available, that would

not alter the fact that the actual suffering would still have to be endured. There is a deeper question than "why?"—namely, "how?" The ultimate question is not "Why has this happened to me?" but "How am I to face it?"...Not an explanation of what has happened, but the grace to...bear it.[13]

Seeking is the spiritual exploration of "why?" Seeking leads us toward the resolution of our grief.

Not unlike most who grieve, after my husband died, I did more seeking than finding. I sought answers within my broken heart, "In the day of my trouble I seek the LORD; in the night my hand is stretched out without wearying" (Psalm 77:2). For many, seeking can become a day and night preoccupation. We lose sleep because we cannot turn off our seeking long enough to rest both our mind and our body. If we are tireless in our seeking, often we lose rather than gain perspective.

Seeking is about measured perseverance, the kind that allows us to pause from time to time and reflect, "Seek the LORD and his strength; seek his presence continually" (Psalm 105:4). When we seek spiritual values—God's comfort, God's love, God's peace—inevitably we find what we are looking for: direction and guidance through our grief.

When we seek, we actualize the presence and power of God, "'Come,' my heart says, 'seek his face!' Your face, LORD, do I seek" (Psalm 27:8). When we seek, we find. God is faithful, "I love those who love me, and those who seek me diligently find me" (Proverbs 8:17).

....

The LORD is good to those who wait for him,
to the soul that seeks him.
Lamentations 3:25

....

FINDING

W hen one we love dies, we search and seek, though not always with the expectation of finding. In the first few days after my husband died, I listened for him to come in the back door each day after work. I expected to hear his car drive into the garage at the usual time. I expected to hear his familiar footsteps bound into the house. I expected to see him—whole and well, full of exuberance, life, and love. I could not find him because he was not there.

When we set out on the journey of searching, seeking, and finding that we call grief, we have no idea what to expect. We do not know what we are searching for, what we are seeking, or what we hope to find. As those who search and seek, we must be prepared to find. What we find may surprise us, delight us, or even shock us.

The journey of grief is unlike our usual plan of travel. Few would consider setting out on a trip without some idea of a route, a destination, and an estimated time of arrival, whether hours, days, or weeks. Recently, I saw a car plastered with souvenir stickers from faraway places. I wondered whether the driver was someone who enjoyed planned adventures or someone who would simply jump in the car and go anywhere—north, south, east, or west. Or perhaps he was only a collector of stickers.

The journey of grief takes us on a circuitous route with pit stops, detours, and setbacks. Along the way, we find what we need to survive the death of our loved one. We find a spiritual place that promises a future with hope. If we are not prepared to find, we stall out on the side of the road.

When we spend time and energy searching and seeking on our journey through grief, what do we expect to find? First, we seek ourself. Often those who grieve find that they have lived part or most of their life in reference to others without thought to who they are as an individual. We never find ourself if we never look to see who we are. When we seek to know ourself, we discover the God-given qualities that make us who we are. When we seek to know ourself, we find the person of stand-alone value and worth that God created us to be. When we find our own true self, we are ready to search, seek, and find life in all of its fullness.

A dear friend whose wife had died three years earlier shared that he had begun to pray for someone to love. He missed the companionship of a partner. He was ready to seek and find joy and new life. He prayed with expectation and hope, "And you will have confidence because there is hope; you will be protected and take your rest in safety" (Job 11:18). A few weeks later, he emailed to say that he had met a lovely woman. They married a few months later. Their union was the fulfillment of his searching and seeking with the expectation of finding. He knew that God had answered his prayer and brought them together. Through the grace of God, he found a new wife with whom he could share the rest of his life. In searching, seeking and finding, we experience the unexpected blessings of grief in the rhythm of God's grace.

Let us therefore approach the throne of grace with boldness,
so that we may receive mercy and find grace to help
in time of need.
Hebrews 4:16

PAUSE TO GRIEVE

My husband and I had the joy of taking a nine-year-old grandson to New York one year to see the sights. The real purpose of the trip was to surround this beloved child with our love and comfort. His parents were divorcing. In the silence of a confused, wounded child, he was grieving the death of family life as he had known it. He needed the stability and assurance that some things in his life would remain unchanged.

He loved animals, so on a warm summer afternoon, we ventured into the Central Park Zoo. To his delight, we discovered the habitat for polar bears. At the time, there were two—Gus and Lily. We smiled and laughed as Gus entertained us with his antics. As he swam and performed, he bumped repeatedly against the glass walls of the tank that contained him. Gus had a large personality that conveyed the joy of being alive.

It was later reported that the decision had been made to euthanize Gus because he was suffering physically with no hope of recovery. Sadness washed over me as I paused to grieve this large, adorable white polar bear, so full of life and energy. I thought of the time when, for a few brief moments, Gus engaged the heart of a small, hurting boy. Gus gave good gifts in his life.

On each anniversary of the events of 9/11/2001, we pause and remember that in a single hour, all of life changed forever. We grieve anew the people who died, the places that are forever changed, the ideals that were tried and tested on that fateful day. For those whose lives were touched personally by death and destruction, grief is refreshed and relived as though it were yesterday. Our enduring national grief commemorates the lives of those who died and honors those who survived. We grieve the loss of our national innocence, the time before 9/11 when suspicion was not at the forefront of everyday life, when travel was not about vigilance and scrutiny, when there was more trust in ourself and in others.

Grief enables us to understand the dimensions and impact of death. When we pause to consider the grief of those in the world we do not know, we cannot help but be more compassionate, empathic human beings. When we read an obituary or death notice, we pause and grieve in quiet solidarity with others. We whisper a prayer for the comfort and strength of people unknown to us, the family members and loved ones of the person who died. Because we know what it is to experience the death of one we love, when we pause to grieve with and for others, we participate in a universal community of compassion for all those who grieve.

Whether death touches us at the core of our being or more on the periphery of our daily existence, the impulse to pause and grieve for everyone and everything that dies to this life is a gift of grief from the grace of God, "The LORD is good to all, and his compassion is over all that he has made" (Psalm 145:9).

We pause and remember. We give thanks for life and love.

Precious in the sight of the LORD is the death of his faithful ones.
Psalm 116:15

LOVE LIGHT

I have loved you with an everlasting love; therefore I have
continued my faithfulness to you.
Jeremiah 31:3

REMEMBRANCE

I t is not unusual to revisit our grief on birthdays and special occasions in our life, "Remember the days of old; consider the years long past" (Deuteronomy 32:7). On my father's birthday, inevitably my thoughts turn both to his life and to his death. It could not be otherwise.

It was one of the great blessings of my life to have this good and godly man as my father. From the moment I was born, it was love at first sight. Through the years, we shared a unique filial relationship—we were friends, confidants, business associates, and allies within a complex, fractured family. My father was my rock; I was his rock. I loved him; he loved me.

When one we love dies, on remembrance days often our thoughts meander through the days and years of our shared history, "I consider the days of old and remember the years of long ago" (Psalm 77:5). Perhaps we gain some new perspective or insight or wisdom that speaks to us about our own life. On remembrance days, we laugh and cry. Often the nature of our relationship—loving and healthy, dysfunctional and unhealthy, or somewhere in between—dictates the emotions we feel.

The greatest gift my father gave me was his unconditional love. By example, he taught me the love of God. His love was constant. His love never changed through the thick and thin of our shared life. This is the love of God that always cares, always disciplines, always protects, always instructs, always nurtures. The unconditional love of God has the power to shape our life, both who we are and who we will become.

The reality of life is that not everyone has a loving father, a loving mother, or a loving spouse. In the twenty-first century, few people are part of an intact, fully functional, nuclear family. When we remember our loved one on occasions that evoke strong emotion, often we struggle to reconcile a past that can never be changed. We observe remembrance days to honor the memory of one we love. If there is little worth remembering, the better part of self-care may be letting go of everyone and everything that has wounded, hurt, or scarred us. On remembrance days, our power lies in releasing the past so that we may live confidently in the present with hope for the future.

Remembrance days draw us into moments of reflection, introspection, and prayer, "For the righteous will never be moved; they will be remembered forever" (Psalm 112:6). When we assess our own life, we see whether we are better for having known and loved the one we now grieve or if our life is a success despite, or perhaps because of, a challenging relationship—life reconsidered, life in perspective, life larger than the sum of all its parts.

We remember, we love. We remember, we cherish. We remember, we let go. We remember, we forgive. We remember, we forget. We remember, we grieve.

....

Remember the former things of old, for I am God, and there is no other; I am God, and there is no one like me.
Isaiah 46:9

....

On Love and Grief

The U.S. Greeting Card Association estimates that approximately 190 million valentines are sent in the United States each year. My husband and I decided to give each other beautiful cards on special occasions rather than gifts. His cards are among my most cherished keepsakes, earthly reminders of our eighteen years of love, romance, and joy. I miss him every day and a thousand times on Sunday. Our love will live in my heart forever, "Love and faithfulness meet together; righteousness and peace kiss each other. Faithfulness springs forth from the earth, and righteousness looks down from heaven" (Psalm 85:10–11 NIV).

For many months after Leighton died, I struggled with the order of love in my life. As I grieved his death, I anguished over whether I had put my love for him above my love for God. I thought about whether there was perhaps some hierarchy of love that I had gotten wrong. One day I realized that love coexists. One love does not exclude another. Love is not either/or.

The divine nature of love is not to limit but encourage, not to control our love but to grow it into greater love, not to possess our love but to share it. God ordains our love. God blesses every expression of love, "God is love" (1 John 4:16). We love because God first loved us.

The exponential power of love is this: the more there is, the more there is to give away. From the experience of grief, we learn more about love. From the experience of death comes a deeper, richer love for our family, friends, and others who need our love. Love is all-inclusive. Love is limitless. Love is infinite. Love never dies.

The assurance of faith is that love is. Love is real. Love is everlasting. Love is eternal. The love we shared with the one now lost to us in death will never die; our love will endure forever. The power of love transcends every circumstance of life, even death, "Love knows no limit to its endurance, no end to its trust, no fading of its hope; it can outlast anything. It is, in fact, the one thing that still stands when all else has fallen" (I Corinthians 13:7–8 PHILLIPS).

> *It always protects, always trusts, always hopes,*
> *always perseveres. Love never fails.*
> *1 Corinthians 13:7–8 NIV*

OCCASIONS

Earth Day, Arbor Day, another wedding anniversary—the occasions of April are heavy laden with all that reminds me of my beloved husband. It is hard to imagine heaven, that better place, when we shared heaven together here on this earth. Ours was a love for all time. German author Goethe expressed it this way, "This is the true measure of love—when we believe that we alone can love, that no one could ever have loved so before us, and that no one will ever love in the same way after us."

On December 28, 1999, the usually peaceful gardens of Versailles in Paris were devastated by a powerful windstorm that uprooted more than ten thousand trees. In just two hours, trees that had grown for over two hundred years were destroyed, trees that had been planted and cultivated since the seventeenth century. The Society of the Friends of Versailles sent an urgent solicitation for contributions to replace the trees. Leighton and I were not members of this organization, but we were certainly friends of Versailles.

It was our custom to mark special occasions in our life with remembrances rather than personal gifts. In honor of Leighton's seventieth birthday, I gave a new tree for the gardens. Months later, an acknowledgment came that identified the location of "his" tree in a particular stand of trees in the garden area of the park.

We visited Versailles on a trip to celebrate our fifteenth wedding anniversary. This would be our final visit to a city in which we had created a lifetime of beautiful memories. We looked for the tree, a small, brave sapling among thousands of new specimens. We found the general area, but not the tree. Though there is not a marker inscribed with his name, I have the pleasure of knowing that something new and green grows in his honor and now in his memory.

We never know when the moment will come that our life will end and be over, "For everything there is a season and a time for every matter under heaven: a time to be born and a time to die" (Ecclesiastes 3:1–2). Even if a relationship seems perfect, it is only for a time. Few among us pause to consider the meaning of forever when marriage vows are spoken "until death do us part." On this side of heaven, we cannot grasp what forever really means. Though death may separate us physically from the one we love, it has no say in forever.

On the occasions of life, I remember and give thanks for having known the joy of a great love. A tree grows in a garden, and life goes on, "Love never ends" (1 Corinthians 13:8 ESV).

Know therefore that the LORD your God is God; he is the faithful God, keeping his covenant of love to a thousand generations of those who love him and keep his commandments.
Deuteronomy 7:9 NIV

REMEMBERING...AGAIN

When one we love dies, our experience of remembering and remembrance mirrors our progress on the journey through grief. The first few years after my husband died, I lived with a sense of irredeemable guilt. I felt that I had failed in my care for him because I could not overcome his cancer through determination and love. Would that illness were so easy to cure, life so easy to restore. For several years, the day on which he died was an occasion of painful recall and recollection. Each year, I scraped back through the grim medical details of what happened to end Leighton's life and the best part of mine.

As his illness progressed, I kept a detailed log of his treatment and related events. Later I transcribed it into a narrative that supported my annual descent into self-recrimination on the anniversary of his death. For many years, it was easier to punish myself for my perceived failure and insufficiency to restore his health than to forgive myself for not being able to save his life. When we are in the eye of the storm, it is easy to confuse our role with that of God.

After much soul-searching, in time I was able to acknowledge to myself that I had done nothing wrong. I did not cause his cancer. I could not cure it. When I gave up on self-reproach, I began to see that, in truth, I had done everything humanly possible to support and sustain his life. Only then was it possible to release the worst of my self-inflicted pain and focus on the sanctity of life and the sacred experience of death.

As the end of his life neared, he sensed that his time was short. He rallied briefly and opened his eyes. In a shining moment, his sweet, adoring spirit returned. It was as though he realized that he had been absent from our life and from me for a long while.

His face shone with gratitude, perhaps because at last I had agreed to let him go. Against the backdrop of his dying, his eyes and spirit drew me into the depths of his soul. I remember and cherish his last words to me, "I love you, I love you, I love you, I love you, I love you, I love you, I love you." He poured his final breath into reaffirming his love for me. These were the last words he ever spoke. The perfect oneness of our parting will live in my heart forever.

I grieve and remember again and again, each time in a different way. Though death is part of our experience of life, death cannot part us. Thanks be to God for the gift of life. Thanks be to God for the gift of eternal love.

Love never dies.
1 Corinthians 13:8 MSG

SEASONS

Spring comes early in Texas. On days heavy with moist, low-lying clouds the scent of new life bursts from every flower and bush. As winter surrenders to spring, my head begins to rattle with the drumbeat of grief.

Love blossomed when Leighton called on a balmy spring evening one year to arrange a first date. We were married the next April. Seventeen years later, a few days after Easter, he was diagnosed with a terminal illness. Ninety days later he died. My beloved father died in April the next year.

Spring evokes memories of the best and worst in life. At this time of year, my heart is powerless to resist the emotions that wash through my spirit, the full range of feelings from sorrow and joy. The challenge of grief is learning to experience seasons of the heart in new ways, whatever the time of year. Life, Love, Death, Grief—the seasons of our soul.

The seasons of nature are an integral part of God's order in the world, "You have made the moon to mark the seasons; the sun knows its time for setting" (Psalm 104:19). Though we grumble when winter is too long, when spring is too rainy, when summer is too hot, when autumn is too cold, there is comfort in the predictability and reliability of the cycle of nature that God created to be the seasons, "Then God said, 'Let the earth put forth vegetation: plants yielding seed and fruit trees of every kind on earth that bear fruit with the seed in it.' And it was so. The earth brought forth vegetation: plants yielding seed of every kind and trees of every kind bearing fruit with the seed in it. And God saw that it was good" (Genesis 1:11–12).

In December one year, the husband of a dear friend died after a traumatic accident and month-long stay in the hospital. Despite her willing spirit and determination to participate in the joy of Christmas, the holiday season is a time of recalled sadness and grief. Winter will always be the season laden with powerful memories of her beloved husband. Winter will always be for her a reminder of the suddenness with which death can change our life. Winter will always recall the heartbreak of slow leave-taking and death. For her, it could not be otherwise. This is the power of love that transcends every season.

The emotional muscle memory of grief often takes us by surprise. A time, a place, a smell, or an event can trigger our emotions and quickly transport us back to our experience of grief. Whatever the season, the heart remembers—always.

When we grieve, we experience seasons that parallel those of nature, though not necessarily in the same order.

- When one we love dies, we live for a while in the bleak midwinter of grief. Our sorrow and pain feel bitterly cold. The winter landscape of our life reflects our desolation. There is little comfort in the winter of our grief.

- As we struggle, grow, and adjust to life without our loved one, we endure the oppressive, challenging heat of summer. At the end of our long hot summer of grief, we accept at last the reality and finality of death.

- In the springtime of grief, we reawaken to life. We open ourself to new possibilities with hope for the future.

- In the autumn of our grief, we enjoy the burnished glow of a deeper, richer faith. The rough edges of grief are worn smooth, our spirit transformed by God's grace.

We learn from the seasons that there is symmetry and order to our experience of grief. We thank God for the seasons of nature that modulate the rhythms of our life. We thank God for the seasons of nature that instruct the seasons of our grief.

For everything there is a season and a time for every matter under heaven: a time to be born and a time to die; ... a time to break down and a time to build up; a time to weep and a time to laugh; a time to mourn and a time to dance; Ecclesiastes 3:1–4

LABOR

When Labor Day rolls around each year, many fire up the grill for an end of summer picnic. Others go to the beach, shop for school supplies, or enjoy a last summer weekend vacation. Officially, Labor Day celebrates the contribution of workers who labor, day in and day out, to ensure the economic productivity of our nation. The work ethic of labor is driven by the pursuit of limitless imagination and human creativity. We see it every day in new technology, new inventions, and new ideas.

Whether you are employed in the traditional workforce, self-employed, under-employed, or work full time making a home, raising children, and being present to the needs of others, work is work. For most of our life, we work at something, even the pursuit of leisure.

One of the inescapable truths of grief is that it is work. For many, grief is hard work. We work at grief so that we may work through it. We work to fix whatever we find within ourself that is broken. Sometimes grief feels like a 24/7 occupation. We cannot seem to lay it down. The hardest thing some of us never do is to rest from grief, "Come to Me, all you who labor and are heavy laden, and I will give you rest. Take My yoke upon you and learn from Me, for I am gentle and lowly in heart, and you will find rest for your souls. For My yoke is easy and My burden is light" (Matthew 11:28–30 NKJV). The Message speaks to our need for rest in this way, "Are you tired? Worn out?...Come to me. Get away with me and you'll recover your life. I'll show you how to take a real rest. Walk with me and work with me—watch how I do it. Learn the unforced rhythms of grace. I won't lay anything heavy or ill-fitting on you. Keep company with me and you'll learn to live freely and lightly" (Matthew 11:28–30 MSG).

When grief is our preoccupation for a while, it is vital to our physical, mental, and emotional health that we put grief aside and take an emotional break from time to time—for an hour, an evening, a day, or a week. If we rest from grief, it does not mean that we forget our loved one. Rather, we allow ourself space to renew our mind, our body, and our spirit. We find our smile and laugh again. We lower our shoulders, relax, and breathe.

Grief waits patiently while we rest. It always shows up again to remind us of what happened. If we take time to care for ourself, when we return to grief, it does not feel quite as insistent as before. It meets us where we are—rested, refreshed, perhaps a little less frazzled. When we take up our grief again, usually we are in a better place.

Grief is our finest, most enduring labor of love. As we remember and honor our loved one, we rebuild our life for the future. Through the labor of grief, we learn the unforced rhythms of grace—the grace of God, the grace of rest for our soul.

On the sixth day God finished the work that he had done, and he rested on the seventh day from all the work that he had done.
Genesis 2:2

SPEED GRIEVING

R ecently I received a letter from a longtime friend whose wife had died recently. They both seemed well when I last saw them together. Her illness, rapid decline, and death shocked her family, especially her husband. He asked for a recommendation on what he might read or do to get over his grief. The outpouring of his heart was agitated; the urgency of his words mirrored his deep distress. He was hurting and wanted to know how to stop the pain. He wanted to be done with grief, sooner rather than later. Clearly, he was trying to speed grieve.

One of the anomalies of grief is that it will not be rushed. Though we would like for our pain to end and be over quickly, there is no such thing as speed grieving. According to poet Henry Taylor, "He that lacks time to mourn, lacks time to mend."[14] Before we can mend and recover from the experience of grief, we must do the work of grief—the solitary, arduous trench work that requires us to go deeper so that we understand the cause and effect of our grief. The resolution of grief is never once-over-lightly, one and done.

A few days after my husband died, I was sitting in a chair in our bedroom, still in shock from his death. Through the murk of unaccustomed brain fog, I realized that I was going to have to go through grief. Intuitively, I knew that there was no way around it. I sensed that grief would be part of my life for many months to come. At the time, I had no idea that pain could be so deep or last so long.

Sometimes in life we are smart enough to know what we do not know. I knew very little about grief. What I did know was that I would have to do the work needed to understand my grief. Over many months, I worked at the hard, thankless task of grief to ensure the survival of my heart and spirit.

As we do the work needed to reconcile ourself to the death of one we love, grief insists that we recognize the emotions that drive our grief. For some, it is sadness, for others it is anger, for others it is fear. What we discover is that there is nothing speedy about untangling our emotions. Yet if we take the time, or make the time, to face our grief, wrestle with it, struggle with it, and at last understand it, slowly we get through grief even as we go through it. This is the reward for doing the slow, steady work of grief.

Many who have experienced the death of a loved one choose a passive form of speed grieving. They simply hang on until they feel that their grief is over. Even if we choose not to enter into our grief actively, more often than not, grief enters into us, whether we like it or not. Imperceptibly it becomes a compelling presence in our mind and heart. As we adjust to life without our loved one, gradually we learn to live alongside grief. The incorporation of the experience of death and grief into our life is a progression that happens slowly over time, never in a burst of calculated speed.

The experience of grief is never resolved overnight. It takes time to absorb the full impact of the death of one we love. Though it is humanly impossible to speed grieve, we are assured that God understands our need for speed, "Incline your ear to me; rescue me speedily. Be a rock of refuge for me, a strong fortress to save me" (Psalm 31:2).

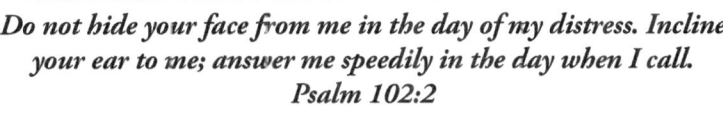

Do not hide your face from me in the day of my distress. Incline your ear to me; answer me speedily in the day when I call.
Psalm 102:2

THE LAND OF HOPE

The psalmist David wrote a loud, noisy song of thanksgiving and praise to God for his deliverance from Saul, "I keep the Lord always before me; because he is at my right hand, I shall not be moved. Therefore my heart is glad, and my soul rejoices; my body also dwells secure" (Psalm 16:8–9 RSV).

Centuries later, the same verse attributed to David is quoted by the Apostle Paul to make a point about the Messiah, "I saw the Lord always before me, for he is at my right hand so that I will not be shaken; therefore my heart was glad, and my tongue rejoiced; moreover, my flesh will live in hope" (Acts 2:25–26).

This verse finds a different voice as interpreted in The Message, "I saw God before me for all time. Nothing can shake me; he's right by my side. I'm glad from the inside out, ecstatic; I've pitched my tent in the land of hope" (Acts 2:25–26 MSG). What is the land of hope? Where is the land of hope? How do we pitch our tent in the land of hope when we grieve the death of one we love?

I went to a big box store one weekend to get a cooler for a road trip. Though I did not find exactly what I was looking for, the search took me through the department for camping gear. I am not a camper but was dazzled by the array of equipment, accessories, and gadgets displayed to make pitching a tent look like fun. A recent newspaper article reported a sharp increase in the number of people who go camping on vacation. I wondered about their destination—the land of hope?

When we grieve, our journey takes us on an expedition through terrain carved from the emotional landscape of our life. We have no idea where we are going or what lies ahead. Before our journey is complete, we encounter rocky hills and valleys, mountains and plateaus, oases and deserts.

On the journey of grief, we trust in God and camp where we are. When we arrive at the end of our journey, just ahead there is a campground where we pitch our tent in the land of hope, "Why are you in despair, my soul? And why are you restless within me? Wait for God, for I will again praise Him for the help of His presence, my God" (Psalm 42:5 NASB).

In the land of hope, we claim God's promise for our life, "'For I know the plans I have for you,' declares the LORD, 'plans to prosper you and not to harm you, plans to give you hope and a future'" (Jeremiah 29:11 NIV).

....

Now hope that is seen is not hope, for who hopes for what one
already sees? But if we hope for what we do not see,
we wait for it with patience.
Romans 8:24–25

....

LIGHT LETS YOU SEE THINGS

My husband and I once had a memorable conversation with a four-year-old grandson about light. We talked about moonlight and sunlight, starlight and candlelight, and several other incarnations of light that seemed to matter in his imaginative mind. When we asked him why light is so important, with the wisdom of a child he answered, "because light lets you see things!" Though we live for a while in darkness when one we love dies, the presence of God lights the way on our journey through grief.

On a trip to New York several years ago, I landed at Newark Airport in New Jersey. From there, the quickest way into the city is through the Holland Tunnel under the Hudson River directly into lower Manhattan. When we drove down the gradual incline into the tunnel for the short ride below ground, I took a breath and knew there was no turning back.

In the middle of the tunnel, a light flashed on top of a maintenance truck a short distance ahead. My mind raced through several worst-case scenarios. Traffic slowed and came to a halt. Then something rather ordinary happened—the driver of the truck hopped out and quickly changed places with a colleague at the mid-way monitoring station, an exchange that took about five seconds. Apparently, it was lunchtime. As we moved forward again and gradually ascended from the depths of the tunnel, at the end was the welcome sight of light.

Moments of travel in a place of relative darkness reminded me that light was there all along, above and outside the tunnel. So it is when we grieve the death of one we love. We descend for a while into a dark place with no turning back. We encounter unexpected stops along the way, until one day we emerge from the darkness of grief. Because we know what it is to live in darkness, we see God's light and understand its power to lead us toward the light of new life.

When we emerge from the tunnel of grief, light lets us see things—the dimensions of our faith, the strength of our spirit, the courage of our heart. Light lets us see God's faithfulness to us when we grieve, "for the LORD will be your everlasting light, and your days of mourning shall be ended" (Isaiah 60:20).

The light shines in the darkness,
and the darkness did not overtake it.
John 1:5

MOVING THROUGH

Over the weekend, I drove to a neighboring city to do a personal errand and have dinner. On the trip home, I was forced to stop for several minutes because of a freight train rumbling through town. Other than municipal light rail service, there is not much passenger train travel in the southwest. Freight trains dominate the rails—the never-in-a-hurry kind that go on for what seems like miles. When the lights began to flash and the crossing arm went down, I stopped my car and prepared to wait.

Though there were too many to count, the train had well over a hundred cars—a mix of box cars, flat cars, storage cars, and silo cars. It lumbered along, gradually slowed, then stopped. I sensed the frustration and impatience of the other drivers. Some peeled off and went down nearby side streets to search for a way around the tracks. In only a few seconds, the train began to move again and at last cleared the intersection without so much as a caboose to mark its end.

As I waited, I thought about how grief moves through our life, much like a slow-moving train. Each freight car of grief is clearly marked—sadness, anger, fear, worry, despair, anxiety, and loneliness to name only a few. If we look under the train, we see the tracks. Simple yet ingenious in design and purpose, tracks determine the pathway of the train, "The human mind plans the way, but the LORD directs the steps" (Proverbs 16:9).

A train track system is engineered using three main components. Two heavy rails set a fixed distance apart support the weight of the train. The gauge of the track—the distance between the inner

– 138 –

edges of the heads of the rails in a track—corresponds precisely to the wheel specifications of the train. The train cannot run without the tracks, and the tracks have no use except to support and direct the pathway of the train. The tracks lead somewhere—east or west, north or south.

Evenly spaced crossties support the tracks that bear the load of the train. The track system is embedded in ballast, small pieces of broken rock packed, then leveled to keep the rails and ties in place. Ballast provides a stable base.

Train tracks are a little like our life when we grieve. Tracks provide the spiritual support of trust and faith, "The LORD is my strength and my shield; in him my heart trusts" (Psalm 28:7). Crossties distribute the weight of our grief through the power of the Holy Spirit, "the fruit of the Spirit is love, joy, peace, patience, kindness, generosity, faithfulness, gentleness, and self-control" (Galatians 5:22–23). The ballast of our grief is laid on the bedrock of our life, "Trust in the LORD forever, for in the LORD GOD you have an everlasting rock" (Isaiah 26:4).

God does not intend for us to sit idling at the railroad crossings of life, wondering and worrying about when life will move forward again or where life will take us. When we grieve, for a while we wait—with frustration and anger or with forbearance and hope. As the train of grief moves slowly through our life, we know from experience that every train ends, with or without a red caboose. When the tracks clear, we are on the move again, eager to reach the final station on our journey through grief.

Trust in the LORD with all your heart,
and do not rely on your own insight.
In all your ways acknowledge him,
and he will make straight your paths.
Proverbs 3:5–6 RSV

GREEN LIGHT

On the way to work one day, something unusual happened—every traffic light was green. I cannot ever remember a daily commute without a single red light. This small coincidence made me feel like it was going to be a good day, like I was somehow in sync with the world and the rhythms of life. But that is not exactly how the day played out. In the middle of the afternoon, an unexpected problem arose that was more than just a metaphoric bump in the road. Though it put the brakes on my morning euphoria, it did not become a head-on collision.

The death of one we love brings us to a standstill. For a while, it seems as though life stops. We feel immobilized, unable to move forward away from the experience of death. As shock abates, we realize that we are at a different place in our experience of grief. Our tears are more controlled, we feel more sadness than sorrow, grief no longer feels like a daily occupation. Though we are apprehensive about the future, we set out in faith on the journey of grief with no idea where it may take us or when we will arrive at our final destination.

Grief is an overland journey. We learn the hard way that grief is a bumpy ride. Like a beginner, we lurch forward then stop. Occasionally, we must slam on the brakes to avoid a fender bender in life. When we are stressed by the desire to navigate grief quickly, we experience emotional road rage. We want to be there, wherever "there" is now.

We set out on what we believe to be the right road, and something happens—a detour, a roadblock, or an obstacle that forces us to take a different direction that leads us to a new, unexpected place.

We know that we are nearing our destination when we see green lights ahead, flashing lights of hope and new life, "Be strong and take heart, all you who hope in the LORD" (Psalm 31:24 NIV).

When one we love dies, even if we are surrounded by a host of family and friends, we feel isolated and alone as we begin our solo journey through grief. Those who have experienced the traumatic, sudden, or tragic death of a loved one often experience grief as personal adversity. If we believe that an institution or individual is responsible for the death of one we love, we want accountability. Seldom, if ever, do side trips down dead-end streets satisfy our desire for justice. There is nowhere that will bring back our loved one. The no-outlet emotions of grief that demand justification lead us nowhere. We are forced to back up and find the right road before we can continue our journey.

Through all the stops and starts and blind alleys of grief, God is present. God is for us, God is with us as we travel the road, potholes and all, on our journey through grief, "I will not fail you or forsake you" (Joshua 1:5).

What then are we to say about these things?
If God is for us, who is against us?
Romans 8:31

CROSSROAD

As we travel the journey of grief, we search for a new direction in life. With the death of one we love, the familiar roadmap of our life is turned upside down—in an instant, north becomes south, east becomes west. We cannot get our bearings.

When we are unable to focus on prayer or anything other than the emotions of grief, often God speaks to us through a single thought or word. For me, God has used the rich imagery of being on a path, "Make me to know your ways, O Lord; teach me your paths" (Psalm 25:4).

The promise is that if we trust God's direction, our path will be made clear to us, "Teach me to do your will, for you are my God. Let your good spirit lead me on a level path" (Psalm 143:10).

On the path through grief, it is not unusual to detour onto personal, unexpected byways—private roads that cause us to revisit the worst of the past, the pain of incomplete relationships, and the emotions we associate with our humanness when we grieve—anger, guilt, and regret to name a few. When we find ourself on a path overgrown with thorny issues from the past, we forgive ourself, forgive others, and move forward in faith, "The way of the righteous is smooth; O Upright One, make the path of the righteous level" (Isaiah 26:7 NASB).

As we navigate the twists and turns of grief, eventually we arrive at a crossroad. If we are distracted by complex, complicated grief, we find ourself on an emotional roundabout and miss the exit. If you find yourself going round and round, struggling in your head and heart with the unresolved emotions of grief, a counselor, therapist, or behavioral health professional may be able to direct you back to the path that leads to life beyond grief.

When one day we reach the crossroad of grief, the intersection of past, present, and future, we stand in the middle of the road. When we pause to look backward, we see the long, winding road we have travelled on our journey through grief. When we look in the other direction, we see the unknown road ahead.

At the crossroad, we must choose our direction, "And when you turn to the right or when you turn to the left, your ears shall hear a word behind you, saying, 'This is the way; walk in it'" (Isaiah 30:21). We can turn around and retrace our steps, revisiting the experience of grief and all that is behind, or we can move beyond the crossroad toward the rest of our life, "Now choose life, so that you and your children may live and that you may love the LORD your God, listen to his voice, and hold fast to him. For the LORD is your life" (Deuteronomy 30:19–20 NIV).

When we choose to move forward, we square our shoulders and march forward to rejoin the world. The promise is that the path beyond the crossroad leads to our God-ordained future, "You must follow exactly the path that the LORD your God has commanded you, so that you may live and that it may go well with you" (Deuteronomy 5:33).

When the crossroad of grief points the way toward our own new lives, we offload the baggage of the past. Our only luggage for the rest of the journey is the backpack that contains the gifts of our grief. Whether or not we realize it, the experience of grief bestows upon us unexpected gifts, many of which we discover for ourself.

It is a sacred responsibility to use the gifts of our grief to help others and in doing so, to serve God. Often we are surprised by how our experience of death and grief can be of help to others. There is always someone who needs our care, our understanding, and our support. There is always someone whose grief is newer than our own.

Because we know what grief feels like, we know how to comfort those whose heart is broken by death, "Blessed be the God and Father of our Lord Jesus Christ, the Father of mercies and the God of all consolation, who consoles us in all our affliction, so that we may be able to console those who are in any affliction with the consolation with which we ourself are consoled by God" (2 Corinthians 1:3–4).

The gifts of grief are similar yet different for each person who grieves. Grief gives us a better understanding of compassion, how to offer it and how to receive it. Grief leads us into a more personal relationship with God. Grief leaves us with an unshakeable conviction that life is worth living.

When we see where we have been on our journey and where we are headed, we know with certainty that God is with us every step of the way, wherever God leads us in our life. On the last occasion that my beloved husband was in the pulpit, he offered this pastoral prayer, "We have come this far by faith, and we will continue to walk with our hand in yours wherever you lead us." God is faithful. In life, in death, in life beyond death, God is with us. Thanks be to God.

. . . for we walk by faith, not by sight.
2 Corinthians 5:7

Moving Forward

As I drove down a neighborhood street one day, I saw a sign that announced the relocation of a local church. There was a directional arrow and this simple statement, "We've grown. We've moved." This unpretentious declaration made me think about the ways we move forward in grief, away from the past toward a future without the one we love.

As we move forward on our journey through grief, we are forced to discover who we are and redefine our individual self apart from our loved one. Many must individuate for the first time in life. This is especially true when the majority of one's life has been spent as part of a couple with a beloved spouse or partner. Without the steady reference point of our loved one, one of the challenges of grief is getting acquainted with ourself, learning who we are without the one we love at our side.

When we individuate, we affirm our own identity as a unique individual created by God. We acknowledge that we have worth and value apart from the one we love and now grieve. Perhaps for the first time in life, we appreciate our God-given qualities, abilities, and gifts, "Then God said, 'Let us make humans in our image, according to our likeness'" (Genesis 1:26).

It is not unusual for the push/pull of grief to feel both confusing and conflicting. Grief offers two options. Either we grow and move forward in life, or we remain rooted in a physical and emotional past that no longer exists. It is a simple, though for many, a complicated choice. When we choose to grow, we move forward and open ourself to possibilities we might never have imagined. If we hold on to the past, we resist growth and succumb to a life of paralyzing self-pity.

As we experience the growing pains of grief, we recognize that certain habits acquired on the journey—chronic sadness, isolation, negativity—are stifling our growth. We feel the need to exercise, to stretch our body, mind, and spirit so that we may grow into the person of stand-alone worth that God created us to be. We ready our heart to live more fully in the present with hope for the future.

Moving forward is the surest way through grief, "but one thing I have laid hold of: forgetting what lies behind and straining forward to what lies ahead, I press on toward the goal, toward the prize of the heavenly call of God in Christ Jesus" (Philippians 3:13–14). In the confidence of our faith, we grieve, we grow, and at last, we move forward away from the past to live the rest of the life God has given us to live beyond this time of grief.

—and may your GOD be with you! Move forward!
2 Chronicles 36:23 MSG

Moving On

After living for twenty-six years in the house my beloved husband and I shared, I decided to move. The decision took several months of thoughtful consideration, deliberation, and intentional prayer before I felt ready to put change in motion. For those who grieve, a major life change—whether a change of residence, a move to a new place, remarriage, or any other catalyst that compels us to adapt and adjust—represents an emotional commitment to the future. For many, it is hard to take leave from the past and move on.

In quiet moments, I think about what I am leaving behind. My husband does not live here anymore. Without him, the house does not feel like home. Without his presence, its emptiness is negative space, a vacuum that cannot be filled. Shadows linger in every room. Though I have maintained and updated the house, it is not my home. It could not be without our love and joy.

Like so many, I am downsizing. I have thought about what part of the past I am taking with me, in the sure knowledge that Leighton's spirit is entirely portable. Who he was, the love we shared, the enduring legacy of his life to mine are forever in my heart. Nothing can change the facts of our life and love together, nothing ever will. The experience of grief empowers us to change, grow, and move forward with expectation for the future.

It is honest to acknowledge our fear when we take a giant leap forward into the unknown. Though the thought of moving somewhere new is a bit intimidating, I think I am ready. I have planned the move and disposed of material things, the flotsam and jetsam accumulated over the years of our life together. I have walked the empty rooms, grieved the void, wept again tears of sweet sadness, and whispered again "if only." I am ready to go.

Moving on in grief is much more than a change of address. It is a change in where we live emotionally and spiritually. Moving on is about accepting the death our loved one. Moving on is about being ready and eager to embrace the rest of our life. We know that we are moving on when we feel different—stronger and better because of our experience of grief. Our spirit has been tried and tested; we have new insight into our soul. When at last we see ourself as survivors, we claim victory over death and grief. We are ready to move on, to live again in fullness of life with joy and hope for the future.

I bless the LORD, who gives me counsel; in the night also my heart instructs me. I keep the LORD always before me; because he is at my right hand, I shall not be moved. Therefore my heart is glad, and my soul rejoices; my body also rests secure.
Psalm 16:7–9

COUNTING THE COST

My father was the sole proprietor of a small commercial construction company in Dallas, Texas for over thirty-five years. Over a professional lifetime, he built over one hundred churches and almost as many schools. He was a good and godly man whose life was grounded in fundamental principles of honesty, integrity, and Christian character.

At a time in history when social consciousness was not a popular concept, my father chose not to construct buildings intended to provide goods and services that would be detrimental to individuals in particular or to society in general. His social conscience was a foundation stone of his business ethos. He demonstrated his commitment to this non-negotiable principle on more than one occasion. I vividly remember a conversation in which he explained with patience and clarity why he would not build a liquor store.

My father was a good estimator both in his work and in his life. After he died in 2005, I found a verse in his Bible that he had marked. In the precise handwriting of a civil engineer, he noted Luke 14:28–30 (ESV) as the Estimator's Verse, "For which of you, desiring to build a tower, does not first sit down and count the cost, whether he has enough to complete it? Otherwise, when he has laid a foundation and is not able to finish, all who see it begin to mock him, saying, 'This man began to build and was not able to finish.'"

When we grieve the death of one we love, sooner or later we realize that if we are to survive and live forward, we must rebuild our life. Like any good estimator, we sit down and count the cost. We question whether we want to make the effort it will take to rebuild.

We consider what we must do to help ourself. We acknowledge the commitment, persistence, and fortitude it will take to reconstruct our life for an unknown future.

Counting the cost is about seeking and finding answers to some of the questions of life and grief. Do I have the kind of faith needed to believe in the future? What do I see when I envision the future? Do I believe that God has a plan for my life beyond this time of grief? Answering the questions of grief is part of the work of rebuilding. When we see God's plan for our future unfolding, our faith grows,

> "So we do not lose heart. Though our outer nature is wasting away, our inner nature is being renewed every day. For this slight momentary affliction is preparing for us an eternal weight of glory beyond all comparison, because we look not to the things that are seen but to the things that are unseen; for the things that are seen are transient, but the things that are unseen are eternal. (2 Corinthians 4:16–18 RSV)

As we excavate the past and pour a new foundation for the remainder of our life, we roll up our sleeves and finish the work of grief, "According to the grace of God given to me, like a wise master builder I laid a foundation, and someone else is building on it. Let each builder choose with care how to build on it" (1 Corinthians 3:10).

I learned from my father that building is risky business. When we risk our emotional capital and invest our spiritual energy in rebuilding our life, inevitably the reward exceeds our expectation, "Eye has not seen, nor ear heard, Nor have entered into the heart of man The things which God has prepared for those who love Him" (1 Corinthians 2:9 NKJV).

Though we have no idea how long it will take or when we will be finished, with discipline, determination, and single-minded focus on what lies ahead, we do the work to rebuild our life. We count the cost and assess the risk. We reassemble the best of who we are, shaped and transformed by our experience of grief. We dare to hope and dream again. We prepare and plan for the future knowing that in God, the best is yet to be. In faith, we rebuild our life.

For we are God's coworkers, working together;
you are God's field, God's building.
1 Corinthians 3:9

HOPE LIGHT

More than that, we rejoice in our sufferings, knowing that suffering produces endurance, and endurance produces character, and character produces hope, and hope does not disappoint us, because God's love has been poured into our hearts through the Holy Spirit which has been given to us.
Romans 5:3-5 RSV

CLEAN BREAK

I received a note from a friend in which she related the details of a major accident. She was the victim of a hit and run driver and one of her legs was fractured in two places. After surgery, there were complications. She endured another surgery, another hospitalization, and weeks of painful rehabilitation.

I saw her at church one Sunday and admired her courage and determination. Not only did she have an obviously painful limp, her spirit seemed somehow broken. Clearly her experience of vehicular assault had taken its toll on her in many ways. She has a strong sense of style, and I wondered whether she would ever be able to wear her stiletto heels again. The next time I saw her she was wearing sensible flats. In her Christmas note, she acknowledged that the damage was probably permanent and her days of wearing high heels were over. She closed by saying how grateful she was that she still had two legs.

Recently, I was surprised to hear myself characterize my experience of grief for my husband as a "clean break" kind of grief. I had never thought of grief in that way and had to stop and think about what it really meant.

When our heart is broken by the force and power of love, the pain feels almost unbearable. This "clean break" kind of grief is one from which we can recover over time, mostly without undue complication. If our love is strong and true, reassembling the pieces of our life honors the love we shared with the one we now grieve.

The edges of our heart feel ragged where the broken parts are rejoined. We never feel quite as whole as we did before the death of our loved one. Yet we know from experience that when something breaks, we become stronger in our broken places. When we grieve a great love, though for a while our heart feels irreparably broken, through the grace of God, one day our brokenness is transformed and made whole, "I give thanks to you, O Lord my God, with my-whole heart, and I will glorify your name forever" (Psalm 86:12).

When relationships are messy or difficult, often we experience a "compound fracture" kind of grief in which our body and mind feel damaged beyond repair or healing. An experience of grief that is about resentment, bitterness, and anger accumulated over a lifetime affects not only our heart and soul but also our ability to move forward in grief and in life.

This kind of layered, compound grief is often resolved by talking out loud to a confidential therapist or professional trained to listen. When the floodgates of the conscious and subconscious mind are opened and shared with someone who understands the cause and effect of complicated grief, often it is surprising what pours out from somewhere deep within our mind and heart.

I have spent many dark days scraping back through the dysfunctional relationship with my mother. Recently, I came across a note to self: let go of the past. I realized then how much time and energy I had spent struggling to get closure on things in the relationship that would never be resolved—things that could not be reconciled either in life or in death.

In a moment of personal permission, I let go of the hurt and misery that once was but will never be again. Though it would be disingenuous to infer that I never again revisited the painful parts of that broken relationship, letting go is sometimes a process. Letting go is something positive that we can do for ourself. Letting go restores our soul. Letting go is about hope and the future.

Seldom is there a clean break when one we love dies. Because God understands the complex emotions of the human heart, God comforts us with mercy and loving kindness when we suffer the pain of heartbreak in grief, "Gracious is the LORD and righteous; our God is merciful. The LORD protects the simple; when I was brought low, he saved me. Return, O my soul, to your rest, for the LORD has dealt bountifully with you" (Psalm 116:5–7).

When the righteous cry for help, the LORD hears
and rescues them from all their troubles.
Psalm 34:17

GOD WITH US

A few months after the death of my husband I went to Washington, D.C. for an event. I decided to make the most of a three-day visit with some sightseeing. The weather was unseasonably warm for late November, so I walked almost everywhere to see the monuments and visit several museums and historic buildings. Along the National Mall, I paused to read many of the beautifully worded inscriptions on the plaques and markers that dot the grand avenue.

At the World War II Memorial, my hand traced slowly over a bronze relief depicting muddy soldiers fighting in the South Pacific where my own father served for four years. It was a powerful personal experience of remembrance and thanksgiving for his survival. I thought of how God was with him in the foxhole as he recited Psalm 23 for strength and courage. Over the years, he shared with me both his fears and his faith. In a moment of spiritual communion with the past, I was humbled and awed by God's presence and faithfulness to all who have served in the military everywhere, for all time.

At the memorial for fallen veterans who served in the Vietnam War, I found the name of a childhood friend who died in that war. I remembered the heartbreak of his parents at the death of their only son. When I thought about their grief, I grasped the reality of God's comfort for all who have ever grieved throughout all the ages of time. I thought of the countless brave men and women that we remember and honor not only on Memorial Day and Veterans Day but forever in our heart.

In the National Cathedral, I lit a candle, knelt, and whispered a prayer of gratitude for the life and love of my husband. The muted sunlight of a waning autumn day streamed through the magnificent rose window and in that moment the certainty of God's faithfulness penetrated my grief. As I wiped away my tears and went out to rejoin the world, I left strengthened by the power and presence of God, resolved to emerge from the spiritual and emotional isolation of grief.

On that November day, my heart and soul were filled with these spiritual truths:

- God is ageless.
- God is timeless.
- God is unchanging.
- God is for all generations.
- God is from everlasting to everlasting.
- God is eternal.
- God is faithful.

God is at the heart of the unbroken heritage we share with those we love and now grieve. God is with us in our grief. God is faithful to all generations of those who grieve and remember.

But you, O LORD, are enthroned forever;
your name endures to all generations.
Psalm 102:12

THE GARDEN
OF THE HEART

What does the garden of the heart look like, especially as we near the other side of grief? The slow, steady drip of grief has taken its toll on the garden of my heart as year after year, family members have died—the death of both parents from Alzheimer's disease, the sudden illness and unexpected death of my beloved husband. There can be no doubt that the God-given beauty of our soul is affected by death and grief. Though the roots of faith grow deep, the garden of my heart looks more like an untended patch than a cultivated bed. Grief is no gardener.

When we grieve, we neglect the garden of our heart. It becomes overgrown with the weeds of grief—worry, anxiety, fear, anger, sadness, and every other variety of emotional confusion that threatens to overtake our heart when one we love dies. Though the weeds of grief are not found in any gardening book, it helps to identify the things growing in our garden so that we know what needs to be cut back, cleaned out, or gotten rid of altogether. Are there perennial, stubborn dandelions that resemble the long-term weeds of grief? Are there annual, dense patches of crabgrass that resemble the short-lived weeds of grief?

We improve the sad state of our garden when we pull out surface weeds and hack away at those that are more deep-rooted. We garden through grief when we get rid of every weed that has the potential to strangle the seedlings of our growth in grief. We restore the garden of our heart when we tend not only that which is visible above ground but also that which is invisible below the topsoil of our life.

When we grieve, there are dormant times when life seems suspended, when the fertile soil of our life lies fallow. During inactive, passive periods of grief, we wait, ready for whatever may come next. In liminal times of emotional and spiritual quiet, the garden of our heart is nourished not by any external source or stimulant but by the comfort and care of the Holy Spirit, "Receive the Holy Spirit" (John 20:22).

God's first acts of creation included the most beautiful garden of all, "The LORD God took the man and put him in the garden of Eden to till it and keep it" (Genesis 2:15). God envisioned for humankind not a desert of grief, but a garden of joy, "For the LORD will comfort Zion; he will comfort all her waste places and will make her wilderness like Eden, her desert like the garden of the LORD; joy and gladness will be found in her, thanksgiving and the voice of song" (Isaiah 51:3).

After the long cold winter of grief, when spring returns we see the potential for new life in the garden of our heart. We seed our life, tend our garden, and wait. We do the labor of cultivation; God provides the nurture. We watch in wonder as all that is planted grows toward the light of new life, prepared to flourish in beauty in the garden of our heart.

....

The LORD will guide you continually, giving you water
when you are dry and restoring your strength.
You will be like a well-watered garden,
like an ever-flowing spring.
Isaiah 58:11 NLT

....

REFURNISHED

I t is always interesting to see how old things look in a new setting. A different place offers a different perspective. In a new
house, a favorite easy chair or comfortable family sofa may
look tired and a little worn out. Conversely, if something new is
introduced into old surroundings, by comparison, everything else
seems to need a cosmetic update or a fresh coat of paint. We scruti-
nize the setting because something looks wrong, not quite right. We
look for a solution to balance the old with the new.

Whether or not we realize it, we undergo many subtle changes
when we grieve. We refurnish our life not necessarily with furniture
or decorative accessories but with new emotions and different experiences that change us over time. We do the work of refurnishing from
the inside out. We hold on to everything we hold dear. We discard
things from the past that no longer add value to our life. We recycle
what is still useful. We repurpose the substance of our life, adapted
to who we are becoming.

A few months before my husband was diagnosed, we did some
remodeling and redecorating. We selected a warm yellow for the
walls, a color popular at the time. Through the years, we cycled from
white walls to red walls to blue walls. Finally, we decided that all the
walls should be the same color.

A few months after Leighton died, I realized that the color we
had chosen was depressing. It made me sad. It reminded me of the
chaotic time of his illness and death. With single-minded resolve, I
called the painter and selected a different color—white. I was amazed
at the positive effect the change in color had on my spirit. By making

an outward change that reflected light and suggested hope, I refurnished something within my soul that was intangible but very real.

When we grieve, we tend to whitewash over our insecurity and self-doubt. However we choose to paint over our grief, the fact remains that life is forever changed by the death of one we love. If we refurnish, we start fresh. We choose a new style and color palette for the rest of our life. We make bold choices and informed decisions that restore our mental and emotional self-confidence. We dare to imagine a brighter future, "How lovely is your dwelling place, O LORD of hosts! My soul longs, indeed it faints, for the courts of the LORD; my heart and my flesh sing for joy to the living God" (Psalm 84:1–2).

Perhaps we move to a new physical home. Perhaps we stay where we are. Whether we go or stay, home will always be that special place deep within our heart where we commune with the spirit of our loved one.

Refurnishing is transformation. Refurnishing is renewal. Refurnishing honors ourself and all that we cherish and hold dear. Refurnishing affirms that there is life beyond this time of grief.

....

Create in me a clean heart, O God;
and renew a right spirit within me.
Psalm 51:10 KJV

....

A NEW VIEW

I have always loved fireworks. My childish fascination with sparklers changed over the years to the enjoyment of enormous displays that feature the latest pyrotechnics. Fireworks transport me to a place of breathless awe and wonder. They are ancient and ingenious. Their magical effects never fail to pleasure my spirit. The year my husband died, we had planned a trip to Boston for July 4 to see the fireworks there. As I cancelled our reservations, I acknowledged for the first time that he was dying.

On July 4 that year, I longed for any sight of celebration after another discouraging day at the hospital. I stood in the street outside our house on that hot summer night and looked up for any sign of light or life. Only a shadow of smoke wafted through the air, its acrid smell a faint reminder of fireworks over for another year. At the time, the hazy night sky seemed like a metaphor for my life—up in smoke.

A few years later, I moved to the seventh floor of a condominium building. From the balcony, I had a front row seat for the July 4 fireworks display about a half mile away. As twilight turned to evening, I pulled up a chair and sat there in pure delight, dazzled by the brilliance and sparkle of the spectacle. I felt myself grinning, I heard myself laugh out loud. In those few moments on a clear summer night, I received the gift of a new view.

When one we love dies, our view of life necessarily evolves and changes. We see things differently; our view of the world is no longer the same. If we choose to live in the past, our only perspective is that which we see in the rear-view mirror of life. Though we know what happened and experienced it, the past is behind us. We can never go back and recover what once was.

In grief, we feel our way through the present. At the same time, we look toward the future We scan the horizon looking for signs of life and wait until the new view of our life comes into focus, "I waited patiently for the Lord; he inclined to me and heard my cry. He drew me up from the desolate pit, out of the miry bog, and set my feet upon a rock, making my steps secure. He put a new song in my mouth, a song of praise to our God. Many will see and fear and put their trust in the Lord ' (Psalm 40:1–3).

We do not know what we will see when our new view becomes clear, but we are assured that we will recognize it when we see it. Our new view may be in the dawn of peace, the sunrise of joy, the clear blue sky of hope, or the bright star of new love. Our new view is revealed through the grace of God, "For your steadfast love is before my eyes, and I walk in faithfulness to you" (Psalm 26:3).

I am about to do a new thing; now it springs forth; do you not perceive it?
Isaiah 43:19

RECONSTRUCTION

There is usually a bit of deconstruction that goes along with emptying a space—pulling out wall hooks, taking apart beds, unscrewing things that are permanently attached to walls. As I did the final clean-out of my parent's house, I found myself going to the toolbox more than once for a hammer, a screwdriver, or some other task-specific tool. I smiled each time I opened the box and reached for one of my father's tools. He was a builder and considered tools to be part of life's essential equipment. He thought that everyone should have a little tool kit.

As grief progresses through our life, we move from shock and despair to growth and adjustment. As we near acceptance, we sense that over the course of our grief, we have been engaged in the process of reconstructing our life.

Seldom is reconstruction a straight-line experience. Our efforts may be random or intentional. However we go about the work of reconstructing our life, we do it because God is preparing us for the rest of our life, "For every house is built by someone, but the builder of all things is God" (Hebrews 3:4). We do it because we know that the one we love and now grieve would want us to rebuild a new life of meaning and purpose for ourself. We do it because we believe that there is a future with hope, "Surely there is a future, and your hope will not be cut off" (Proverbs 23:18).

When we embrace the idea of reconstruction, we honor the spiritual and emotional certainty that our life has value. The death of one we love does not consign us to the scrap heap of life. Though we are changed by the experience of death and grief, the integrity of who we are remains intact. Our life is worthwhile; our life is worth rebuilding.

The most essential part of any construction is a sound foundation, "The rain came down, the streams rose, and the winds blew and beat against that house; yet it did not fall, because it had its foundation on the rock" (Matthew 7:25 NIV). When we are tried and tested by the death of one we love, the foundation of our life is shaken. We feel for a while as though we have lost everything, that the structure of our life has collapsed. Whatever challenges we encounter when we grieve, we depend on God, the bedrock of our soul. God is our sure foundation. God is never shaken and never moved, "Cast your burdenon the LORD, and he will sustain you; he will never permit the righteous to be moved" (Psalm 55:22).

Grief teaches us first-hand many fundamentals of engineering and practical guidelines for reconstructing our life.

- There is a plan to follow. First, we envision a design. Then we begin to rebuild, following specified construction steps that must occur in sequence. If our plan is altered by circumstance, we revise the design, make adjustments, and continue to rebuild.

- Reconstruction is hard work. There is no skill set for grief. The work of reconstruction is labor-intensive and emotionally exhausting. We use experience as our building blocks and reconstruct our life on the foundation of faith, "Unless the LORD builds the house, those who build it labor in vain" (Psalm 127:1).

- Construction is handwork. Though heavy machinery is used to clear, dig, and hoist, the work of construction is done by human beings. Hands guide the saw that cuts materials to measure, hands direct the nail gun to connect and affix materials, hands direct the riveter that fastens the whole in place. When we grieve, we rebuild our life one piece at a time with the support of spiritual resources. We read, pray, meditate, and listen for God's instruction,

"I will instruct you and teach you the way you should go;
I will counsel you with my eye upon you" (Psalm 32:8).

- Reconstruction is the work of self-nurture. We honor our
  body with proper care. We work to ensure our physical
  and emotional health and well-being. When we rebuild
  our life, we eliminate destructive behaviors. We affirm
  ourself as the person God created us to be. We recognize
  our unique God-given talents and gifts and offer them in
  service to God and others.

Reconstruction is the work of faith. When we rebuild our life,
we build on the Rock, "The LORD is my rock, my fortress, and my
deliverer, my God, my rock in whom I take refuge, my shield, and
the horn of my salvation, my stronghold" (Psalm 18:2).

....

*I will show you what someone is like who comes to me, hears my
words, and acts on them. That one is like a man building a house
who dug deeply and laid the foundation on rock; when a flood
arose, the river burst against that house but could not shake it
because it had been well built.*
Luke 6:47–48

....

REBUILDING

About two miles away from where I grew up, there was a Mrs. Baird's bakery. The large factory was an urban anomaly for Dallas, Texas because it was located in an upscale residential neighborhood across from Southern Methodist University. Though the site was part of the local landscape, somehow a manufacturing plant did not fit in.

In a full-page newspaper ad on November 2, 1953, Mrs. Baird's announced the opening of its new, fully-automated bakery. At the time, it was the world's largest bread factory. The ad invited the public to bring the whole family and come for a tour to observe firsthand the commercial process for making bread. It also suggested that visitors wear walking shoes for the quarter-mile loop through the plant.

A few months later, on a balmy Friday evening, our family took the tour. There were no visitor regulations—no hair nets, gloves, or special clothing required. I am certain that I had no walking shoes. Likely, my father carried me in his arms for most or part of the quarter mile tour. Though I have little memory of the actual tour, what I do remember is the unforgettable smell and taste of freshly baked bread.

At the end of the production line, loaves of fresh white bread emerged from the oven. At the time there was only white bread, or "light" bread as it is called in some parts of Texas. No wheat, whole grain, or designer bread, only white bread—hot, sliced, and ready to be packaged. As we watched in amazement, the tour guide deftly pulled a loaf of bread from the conveyor belt and held it aloft so that everyone could see this miracle of modern baking. In the drama of the moment, we felt his pride in the tradition of Mrs. Baird's bread.

As a reward for our attention and interest, he took the loaf of hot bread, separated its thick slices, and slathered each with real butter before offering a whole piece to each person in the group. No sample sizes or sharing. I remember the delight of having a whole piece of hot bread to eat all by myself. The entire experience was one of wonder and pure joy for a small, impressionable child.

During the second half of the twentieth century, the company prospered. The entire community knew when bread was in the oven. Its yeasty aroma filled the air with clockwork regularity every day of the week. The smell of freshly baked bread became part of community lore for an entire generation.

In 1998, Mrs. Baird's was sold to Grupo Industrial Bimbo, Mexico's largest baker and food company. The decision was made to close the Dallas factory. Over time, it had become functionally obsolete. The last loaves of bread were baked in 2002. The passing of Mrs. Baird's bakery was the end of an era. The community mourned the loss of an institution.

When the property was sold to Southern Methodist University, the site was cleared for future development. Rather than implode the low-rise factory, it was not so much torn down as it was deconstructed. Likely there were environmental issues of concern with such an old factory. This was a labor-intensive process. Over several weeks, the robust steel and concrete construction of the building was carefully dismantled. A wrecking ball pounded the walls with unrelenting persistence. As the building began to fall, structural materials were sorted into piles of twisted salvage and recyclable materials. That which could not be reused or repurposed was hauled away by giant dump trucks—load by load, day after day.

When the work was finished, the last vestiges of a neighborhood landmark were gone. The vacant lot was levelled and prepared for new construction. The pie-shaped site seemed clean and vast, an illusion of perspective and perception. For a while, an earthmover with a front-end loader sat idle in the middle of the lot. It seemed to proclaim, "Our work is finished. Look what we have done." A water standpipe seemed to survey the horizon in search of the future. Birds pecked through freshly turned soil in search of nourishment. A wobbly construction fence rippled and swayed around the irregular perimeter, its outline a suggestion of all that was yet to be.

This chronicle of productivity, change, deconstruction, and rebuilding is a metaphor for life. As with the factory, the doors open, and life begins. We put on our walking shoes and take the tour. We savor the joy of living when our daily bread is spread with the buttery goodness of love. We are productive and useful until change happens, progress stops, and life as we have known it unceremoniously grinds to a halt. When we grieve the death of one we love, for a while we experience deconstruction in our life, "a time to search and a time to give up" (Ecclesiastes 3:6 NIV).

Deconstruction is unbuilding in order to rebuild, "a time to tear down and a time to build" (Ecclesiastes 3:3 NIV). We sort through the rubble, "a time to scatter stones and a time to gather them" (Ecclesiastes 3:5 NIV). We keep all that is useful and discard that which is not, "a time to keep and a time to throw away" (Ecclesiastes 3:6 NIV). The ground perspective of our life is forever changed by the death of one we love. Our future awaits on the level ground of a life rebuilt in hope.

Though we no longer bake fresh bread, we are ready to rebuild, "There is a time for everything, and a season for every activity under the heavens" (Ecclesiastes 3:1 NIV).

....

It shall be said, "Buildup, buildup, prepare the way;
remove every obstruction from my people's way."
Isaiah 57:14

....

UNISON

Most professional musicians know that unison is difficult to achieve. Before the beginning of every concert or performance, there is a pause, a short time dedicated to tuning the instruments to the same pitch. Usually an oboist plays A440, the internationally recognized standard for musical pitch: the 440 Hz tone that corresponds to the musical note A above middle C. Orchestra members make whatever adjustments are needed so that every instrument is tuned to the same pitch. At least in theory, the result is perfectly tuned sound, the place where unison begins.

Unison singing is more difficult. Every person, every voice, and every ear is different. The effect of voices singing in unison is achieved only through listening and musical accommodation by adapting to the sound of others. A collective sound that approximates that of a single voice demands the submission of each single voice to the unison of the larger whole.

Grief is perhaps the most atonal experience in all of life. When one we love dies, the unison of relationship is disrupted. The harmony of our spirit becomes a cacophony of dissonant emotions. At once, we are out of tune with ourself and those we love, sometimes even with God. Surrounded by the white noise of grief, we express the discord within us as anger, fear, guilt, and resentment. When we grieve, we are compelled to attune our life to the clamor of world. Though the music of our life stops for a while when one we love dies, the unison of love resonates within our heart forever.

When all is said and done, the inmost desire of our heart is to be at one with God, to live in unison with the indwelling presence of the Holy Spirit. When our soul is dissonant, when we feel out of tune with all that is spiritual, lasting, and real, often it is difficult to still our heart and find our voice to pray, "By day the LORD commands his steadfast love, and at night his song is with me, a prayer to the God of my life" (Psalm 42:8).

Spiritual unison is the work of fine tuning our spirit with the heart of God, "You have made known to me the ways of life; you will make me full of gladness with your presence" (Acts 2:28). When we are at one with God, we are in unison with life.

My presence will go with you, and I will give you rest.
Exodus 33:14

RECOVERY

There is something about grief that seems at odds with the idea of recovery. Recovery suggests that somehow we are going to get back what death has taken away. Recovery seems more like a vague aspiration when we realize that one we love will never see a child grow up, that a parent will not be at a child's graduation or wedding, or that a beloved grandmother will never again bake her famous cherry pie.

Recovery describes the spiritual and emotional reclamation of our life. We know that we are recovering when our self-confidence is renewed. We know that we are recovering when we find satisfaction in life again. We know that we are well on the way to the other side of grief when we hear ourself say "I am better," "I want to live," "Life is good," or other self-talk that is positive and affirmative. If we do all we can to care for ourself physically, mentally, emotionally, and spiritually, there is every chance that we will recover from the experience of grief.

A few months after my husband died, I read a magazine article by a woman who was also grieving the death of her husband. She described her experience of pain, then went on to say that she found recovery at a spa. I paused to consider and question. Though the experience of grief is individual and personal, could recovery really be achieved with a massage?

Likely her body felt better after some therapeutic treatments and a few days' rest. The hard truth of grief is that our spirit and soul do not recover from grief at a spa, at the mall, or in some distant place far from home. Though these places offer a temporary respite from grief, they are far removed from the experience of spiritual and emotional recovery when one we love dies.

Often we reach for so-called remedies for grief. We soon discover that recovery is not found in a bottle of cosmetics, alcohol, or pharmaceuticals, or in a grocery store or restaurant, or in anything before us on the table. Momentary, short-lived, feel better panaceas do little or nothing to help us recover from grief. In essence, recovery is about discovery. It is about getting acquainted or reacquainted with our own best self. Recovery lies within the resolve to do better and be better because of our experience of grief.

If we believe that it is possible to recover from grief, we want to know what we need to do to make it happen. Though there is no guarantee that our recovery will be full or complete, when we desire positive change in our life, there is every possibility that we will be restored unto ourself. We know that we are recovering when we become less tearful and less fearful. We know that we are recovering when we begin to feel stronger. We know that we are recovering when we are more engaged and enthusiastic about life. This is what recovery feels like to many.

How we recover is as individual and personal as each person and each experience of grief. Consider these possibilities for recovery:

- Think about new ways to pray—for yourself and for others. Pray for renewal and transformation, "Rejoice in hope, be patient in suffering, persevere in prayer" (Romans 12:12 NRSV).

- Be thankful for who you are and the gift of life.

- Resolve to complain less, especially about that which can never be changed.

- Read for grief understanding and spiritual enrichment.

- Find your smile and laugh out loud.

- Stay connected to the world—the world is not waiting on you or for you.

- Reach out to others to relieve your isolation and loneliness.

- Be grateful for the steadfast love and faithfulness of God.

- Trust that God has a perfect plan for your future.

- Continue in faith, "for whatever is born of God conquers the world. And this is the victory that conquers the world, our faith" (1 John 5:4).

When one we love dies, often we allow our relationship to define us—who we are and how we live. If life is qualified only by the death of one we love, we allow the past to be the primary stakeholder in our future. As we recover, we begin to see that what we have experienced is part of our history and the permanent landscape of our life—the good, the bad, the beautiful, and all the rest. Though the past will always be, recovery is about relaxing into the present with a view to the future.

When we grieve, it is tempting to give up on hope. For a while, it seems as though everything we ever hoped for died along with our loved one. Most find that hope is incremental. Hope builds on hope; hope thrives on hope. When we want to be better, when we want to recover from grief, we start small and learn again to hope. We discover within our grief that for which we should hope. As we near the end of our journey through grief, hope looks different and feels different.

We experience recovery when our heart soars heavenward, listening for whispers of love from the one now lost to us in death. As the end of grief nears, there is perhaps no more powerful moment of perfect peace than when we know without doubt that the love we shared with the one now lost to us in death is alive and well, fully present in our heart. We hear a familiar voice say, "I love you" and know that all is well.

I am the resurrection and the life. Those who believe in me, even though they die, will live, and everyone who lives and believes in me will never die. Do you believe this?
John 11:25–26

SOARING

ecently, I took a vacation, the first in several years. Usually, travel is for business with a little pleasure tucked in somewhere along the way. During the years that I was a primary caregiver, I never left town without feeling like a large piano was strapped to my back. Travel is not always enjoyable when you are on call, always in readiness mode waiting for the next event or emergency, aware that at any moment your plans could change.

After clearing security and a slight delay in boarding, I found my seat and realized that I had nothing to do except relax. It was an unaccustomed luxury to be going somewhere without a load of duty and responsibility along for the ride. As the plane took off and began its slow ascent, I felt my spirit begin to soar.

I was alive. I had survived the years of elder care and the death of my beloved husband. I felt like I was at last on the way to a new place in my life with my heart and soul relatively intact. I felt ready to live again, whatever that might be, however it might happen. I wanted to soar.

Consider the awe-inspiring sight of an eagle soaring through the sky. At liftoff, the bird spreads its wings and takes a leap. During the first few wingbeats, the eagle tucks its legs, assuming the streamlined shape needed for efficient flight. Once airborne, in an economy of energy, the eagle repeats a flap-flap-glide sequence. It does not rely on continuous flapping to gain altitude but on the effect of rising air currents. The lifting power of its outstretched wings is an aerodynamic phenomenon that allows an eagle to stay aloft longer than any other bird. An eagle flies by soaring.

As those who grieve, we long to soar again—to ascend from the depths of grief, reach new heights, and soar in effortless, joyful flight. One of the challenges of grief is waiting—waiting on God, waiting to feel better, waiting for life to unfold. If we wait for everything to return to the way it was before the death of our loved one, we wait in vain for something that will never happen. If we wait for the future and allow ourself to dream and imagine what might lie ahead, we are waiting to soar.

When we wait for God, our strength is renewed. In the certainty that God's lifting power is sufficient to soar, our spirit ascends upward toward God,

> Bless the LORD, O my soul, and all that is within me, bless his holy name. Bless the LORD, O my soul, and do not forget all his benefits—who forgives all your iniquity, who heals all your diseases, who redeems your life from the Pit, who crowns you with steadfast love and mercy, who satisfies you with good as long as you live so that your youth is renewed like the eagle's. (Psalm 103:1–5)

....

But those who wait upon GOD get fresh strength. They spread their wings and soar like eagles, They run and don't get tired, they walk and don't lag behind.
Isaiah 40:31 MSG

....

HAPPINESS

As grief slowly moves beyond the pain of loss and sadness, often we ask ourself, "Will I ever be happy again?" Usually our answer is qualified, "I might be happy again one day if only something would happen that would make me feel better again."

"Blessed are those who mourn, for they will be comforted" (Matthew 5:4). This promise is somewhat counterintuitive. It assures us that because we mourn, we will be blessed or happy. But how do we reconcile blessedness and mourning with comfort and happiness? The promise is that God will comfort us when we mourn. Through God's comfort, we are blessed or happy. Though this thought process makes sense in principle, often our grief equation does not quite add up to happiness.

Because mourning is the expression of our inmost sorrow, grief insists that we mourn before we are blessed with comfort or happiness. Happiness is the reward. It is the result of something that we have done; we have mourned. Sometimes happiness enters our life through a side door and comes to us by indirection, "You're blessed when you feel you've lost what is most dear to you. Only then can you be embraced by the One most dear to you" (Matthew 5:4 MSG).

The experience of grief teaches us that happiness is a by-product of our inner stability rather than a reflection of our outward security. When we grieve, we explore and discover, perhaps for the first time in our life, the extent of our stability apart from all the things that define our outward security. We search our soul. We get acquainted with ourself in a different way at a spiritual and emotional place removed from the things of this world. We experience deep, soul-satisfying happiness when our inner stability prevails over every pretense of outward security. Happiness begins where we are. Happiness comes from within the heart. Authentic happiness is an inside story.

On a Friday afternoon at the end of a long week, I was sitting at my desk writing some letters and signing a few checks. It was quiet. The day was bright; the outside world seemed peaceful and calm. As I sat for a few moments enjoying the sunlight, I realized that for the first time in a long while I felt happy. I was happy to have work to do, I was happy to be in pleasant surroundings, I was happy to have time to reflect on the events of the past year. I was blessed by a feeling of spiritual happiness, which had everything to do with inner peace.

As I reflected later on this experience of momentary happiness, what I discovered is that really it was more about joy—the joy of feeling useful, joy that my life again had meaning and purpose, joy that my years of sadness and grief were at last at an end. One of the lessons we learn from grief is the difference between here-today-gone-tomorrow happiness and deep, abiding joy, "Whenever you face trials of any kind, consider it nothing but joy, because you know that the testing of your faith produces endurance; and let endurance have its full effect, so that you may be mature and complete, lacking in nothing" (James 1:2–3).

Joy has an indescribable quality all its own. Joy is profound gratitude. Joy is the balance of peace and hope within our heart. Joy is the outcome of love, even in the face of death. At the end of the day, joy is the ultimate quest of our grief journey. Thanks be to God for the gift and blessing of joy.

....

Happy are people who grieve, because they will be made glad.
Matthew 5:4 CEB

....

RESTORATION

I f you are fascinated or entertained by television programs that follow the renovation and restoration of homes, likely you have seen the dramatic moment when a homeowner or builder raises a sledgehammer to begin demolition. After that, things get worse before they get better, until the project begins to take on new function and form in the work of restoration. The process of restoration is an apt metaphor for the experience of grief. When one we love dies, we experience demolition, repairs, upgrades, and at last restoration.

A beloved scripture many associate with grief is Psalm 23. In a few short verses, this beautiful song of David eloquently describes our journey through grief, "The LORD is my shepherd, I shall not want; he makes me lie down in green pastures. He leads me beside still waters; he restores my soul. He leads me in paths of righteousness for his name's sake" (Psalm 23:1–3 RSV). We are told who we will follow and assured that God is sufficient to our every need. We are told what to expect along the way—a place to rest and time to reflect. We are assured that God will restore our soul. God leads us in a way that reveals God's love for humankind.

We are assured that God is with us on the journey of grief, "Even though I walk through the valley of the shadow of death, I fear no evil; for thou art with me; thy rod and thy staff, they comfort me" (Psalm 23:4 RSV). God does not prevent us from going through the experience of the death of one we love. Rather, God walks with us through the valley of the shadow of death. Because God is present to comfort and protect us, we do not need to be fearful, whatever happens, wherever we are.

At the end of our grief journey, we claim the blessing of restoration, "Surely goodness and mercy shall follow me all the days of my life; and I shall dwell in the house of the LORD for ever" (Psalm 23:6 RSV). Our whole life long, we are pursued by God's love. When we grieve, we live into God's grace, "For in him we live and move and have our being" (Acts 17:28 NIV).

When the work of restoration is at last complete, the experience of grief no longer defines us. Rather it becomes part of who we are. We will never forget where we have been. We will never forget our loved one.

As with any restoration, the pieces of our life have been rearranged and reordered. We do not look the same or feel the same as we once did. We have struggled and at last prevailed over death and grief. Through the grace of God, we are restored from without and within. Through the grace of God, we are restored to life and made whole again.

....

Restore us to yourself, O LORD, that we may be restored;
renew our days as of old.
Lamentations 5:21

....

VIEW FROM THE MOUNTAIN

From time to time, my husband preached on what the Bible has to say about daily living. In one sermon, he talked about the highs and lows of everyday life in contrast to the mountaintop experiences we all have from time to time. As ordinary people, seldom do we sustain the euphoria of the mountaintop in our daily life.

Leighton and I lived on the mountaintop of joy in our married life together. Every day was a celebration of love. When he died, a part of me died. In the finality of a single breath, my love for life and hope for the future seemed gone. With his death, my joy died, too.

If we have experienced the top of life's most beautiful mountain, the death of one we love feels like a free-fall into the depths of grief. When our mountain crumbles, for a while every day seems like an uphill struggle to climb out of the valley of the shadow of death. We are daunted by the rugged terrain of life without our loved one at our side. We have no idea how to scale the heights and survive.

On a summer vacation to Colorado the year before he died, Leighton and I visited Pike's Peak, a fourteen-thousand-foot elevation with a breathtaking vista that on a clear day seems to offer a view of all the world. It was a perfect day, a sparkling day that filled me with excitement and gratitude for the bounty of love and joy that filled our life.

As we stood next to each other, he slipped his hand into mine. It was soft and warm and strong. In that exquisite moment of shared quiet and spiritual union, we were alive to each other and to all of life. In the joy of a mountaintop moment, hand in hand we read the inscription on a plaque commemorating the poem "America the Beautiful" by Katherine Lee Bates. Her visit to the mountain in 1893 inspired her to write these words, "All the wonder of America seemed displayed there, with the sea-like expanse."[15]

Our shared oneness at that peaceful place on a glorious summer day was a cameo moment in life when we take a mental picture and create a lasting memory in our heart. I remember the smell, the warmth, and the perfection of God's creation on that glistening day of love and life, "and if I have a faith that can move mountains, but do not have love, I am nothing" (1 Corinthians 13:2 NIV).

On the Sunday before July 4 one year, the choir sang the first verse of "America the Beautiful" as a choral benediction. In an unexpected moment of grief recalled, the power of that mountaintop memory flooded my heart. Tears filled my eyes, I felt the warmth of Leighton's hand slip into mine, and I was transported to a day and place and a sacred experience of love.

Thanks be to God for the gift of love. Thanks be to God for the gift of life, beautiful life.

....

For the mountains may depart and the hills be removed, but my steadfast love shall not depart from you, and my covenant of peace shall not be removed, says the LORD, who has compassion on you.
Isaiah 54:10

....

O love of God, how strong and true!
Eternal, and yet ever new;
Uncomprehended and unbought,
Beyond all knowledge and all thought.

O love of God, how deep and great!
Far deeper than man's deepest hate;
Self-fed, self-kindled, like the light,
Changeless, eternal, infinite.

O heavenly love, how precious still,
In days of weariness and ill!
In nights of pain and helplessness,
To heal, to comfort, and to bless.

O wide embracing, wondrous love,
We read thee in the sky above,
We read thee in the earth below,
In seas that swell, and streams that flow.

We read thee best in Him who came
To bear for us the cross of shame;
Sent by the Father from on high,
Our life to live, our death to die.

We read thy power to bless and save
Even in the darkness of the grave;
Still more in resurrection light,
We read the fullness of thy might.

O love of God, our shield and stay
Through all the perils of our way!
Eternal love, in thee we rest
Forever safe, forever blest.[16]

THE OTHER SIDE
OF GRIEF

Occasionally, someone whose grief is much newer than mine asks a hope-filled question about what life is like on the other side of grief. Usually, there is quiet urgency in their need for assurance that there is something beyond their momentary pain. They want to know whether they will ever experience joy again in life and whether life will ever again be more about hope and less about grief.

Often, we wonder whether the experience of grief will somehow leave us permanently damaged. Seldom do we consider the possibility that grief might entrust us with some gifts along the way. It is almost impossible to imagine that grief might benefit us and bear fruit in our life, "My Father is glorified by this, that you bear much fruit" (John 15:8). Reconciling our experience of death with the grace of grief leads us slowly but surely to the other side of grief.

When we take a backward glance to see where we have been and what we have been through, often we find that we are rounder spiritually and more mature in our faith. We see that we are more agile emotionally and more adaptable than we were before the death of our loved one. We have grown, we have adjusted, we have changed. We are more resilient, more understanding, more forgiving, and more tolerant of others. Grief can have a positive, lasting effect on our soul and spirit if we open our heart to receive its gifts.

If we arrive at the other side of grief, are we suddenly over the rainbow? No, life is not that simple. We are not instantly better, though we are certainly in a better place. We glory in the light reflected through the rainbow because we have lived for a while in the darkness of grief. We rejoice in the vibrant colors of the spectrum, grateful for eyes to see brilliant hues that suggest new life. We recognize in its perfect arc the symmetry of life and death.

From the limited sightline of our mortality, on the other side of grief we perceive the dimensions of God's love, "I pray that you may have the power to comprehend, with all the saints, what is the breadth and length and height and depth and to know the love of Christ that surpasses knowledge, so that you may be filled with all the fullness of God" (Ephesians 3:18–19).

After we have grieved for a while, however long that may be, the light of new life beckons us into the future on the other side of grief. Thanks be to God for the victory over death. Thanks be to God for the eternal light of love. Thanks be to God for life beyond the broken heart.

....

Then your light will break forth like the dawn, and your healing will quickly appear; then your righteousness will go before you, and the glory of the LORD will be your rear guard. Then you will call, and the LORD will answer; you will cry for help, and he will say:

Here am I.
Isaiah 58:8–9 NIV

....

NOTES

¹ Helen Keller, "Three Days to See," *The Atlantic*, January 1933, pp. 36–40.

² George Philipp Schmidt, "The Wanderer," *Taschenbuch zum geselligen Vergnügen* (Leipzig, Germany: Wilhelm Gottlieb Becker, 1808), 191.

³ Edna St. Vincent Millay, as quoted in Nancy Milford, *Savage Beauty: The Life of Edna St. Vincent Millay* (New York: Random House, 2002), 328.

⁴ Paul David Tripp, *New Morning Mercies* (Wheaton, IL: Crossway, 2014), 2/11.

⁵ Robert Burns, "To a Mouse, on Turning Her Up in Her Nest With the Plough, November, 1785," *Poems, Chiefly in the Scottish Dialect*, Kilmarnock Edition (Kilmarnock, Scotland: John Wilson, 1786), 138.

⁶ C.S. Lewis, *A Grief Observed* (San Francisco: HarperCollins, 1961), 3.

⁷ Edmund Burke, *A Philosophical Inquiry into the Origin of Our Ideas of the Sublime and Beautiful* (New York: Oxford University Press, 2008), 53.

[8] Henri Nouwen, *Turn My Mourning Into Dancing* (Nashville: Thomas Nelson, 2001), 80.

[9] Joyce Rupp, *May I Have This Dance?* (Notre Dame, IN: Ave Maria Press, 2007), 34.

[10] Søren Kierkegaard, "Philosophy and Science," *The Diary of Søren Kierkegaard*, (New York: Citadel Press, 1960) pt. 5, set 4, no. 136.

[11] Leighton K. Farrell, "The Will of God," sermon preached at Highland Park United Methodist Church, Dallas, TX, September 30, 1984.

[12] John Newton and William Cowper "Faith's Review and Expectation," *Olney Hymns* (Olney, Buckinghamshire, England: 1779), 53.

[13] Leighton K. Farrell, *Cries from the Cross* (Nashville: Abingdon Press, 1994), 46–47.

[14] H. Henry Taylor, *Philip Van Artevelde* (1834), Part 1, Act 1, Scene 5.

[15] See http://adm2.elpasoco.com/epchome/plaque.asp.

[16] Horatius Bonar, *Hymns of Faith and Hope* (London: James Nesbit, 1861), 52–54.

SCAN HERE to learn more about
Invite Ministries—created to invite people to a deeper
faith and living relationship with Jesus Christ

www.ingramcontent.com/pod-product-compliance
Lightning Source LLC
Chambersburg PA
CBHW020239130626
46549CB00005B/1966